DECODING THE DIGITAL JUNGLE

**VIKAS CHAWLA
DAVID APPASAMY
NANDITA RAMAN**

INDIA • SINGAPORE • MALAYSIA

Notion Press

No.8, 3rd Cross Street,
CIT Colony, Mylapore,
Chennai, Tamil Nadu – 600004

First Published by Notion Press 2021
Copyright © Vikas Chawla, David Appasamy, Nandita Raman 2021
All Rights Reserved.

ISBN 978-1-63832-502-4

This book has been published with all efforts taken to make the material error-free after the consent of the author. However, the author and the publisher do not assume and hereby disclaim any liability to any party for any loss, damage, or disruption caused by errors or omissions, whether such errors or omissions result from negligence, accident, or any other cause.

While every effort has been made to avoid any mistake or omission, this publication is being sold on the condition and understanding that neither the author nor the publishers or printers would be liable in any manner to any person by reason of any mistake or omission in this publication or for any action taken or omitted to be taken or advice rendered or accepted on the basis of this work. For any defect in printing or binding the publishers will be liable only to replace the defective copy by another copy of this work then available.

Contents

Book Outline	5
Introduction	7
Upper Funnel: Building Your Brand Online	9

Chapter 1 The Rallying Cry for Your Herd: Setting
             Your Marketing Objective   11
Chapter 2 The Making of a Main Attraction:
             Establishing a Brand Persona   18
Chapter 3 The Leap of Faith: Moving from Offline to Online   30
Chapter 4 Demarcating Your Territory: The Foundation
             of a Strong Digital Presence   38
Chapter 5 Adaptation and Evolution: The Changing Consumer   44
Chapter 6 Mirroring Bird Calls: Personalization
             of the Consumer Journey   50

Middle Funnel: Earning Your Audiences' Trust and
Imparting more Knowledge on what Your Brand has to Offer   57

Part I: Owned Media   59

Chapter 7 Summoning the Pack: Improving Findability
             with SEO and Content   61
Chapter 8 Navigating the Skies: Building Seamless
             User Experience   73

Chapter 9 Conducting the Orchestra: Storytelling Through Videos	79
Chapter 10 Building a Formidable Network: Crafting a Social Media Strategy	86

Part II: Paid Media — 93

Chapter 11 Spotting the Watering Holes: Choosing the Right Platforms to Target	95
Chapter 12 Building Coalitions and Advocates: The Power of Influencer Marketing	101
Lower Funnel: Going the Extra Mile to Convert Potential Customers into a Loyal Customer, and Driving ROI to Meet Your Goals	108
Chapter 13 Responding to Signals: Intent-Based Targeting	109
Chapter 14 Hidden Sanctuaries: Emerging Digital Ecosystems	119
Chapter 15 Tracking Paw Prints in the Ground: Measuring Results from Digital	127
Chapter 16 Bridging the Great Divide: Online-Offline Integration	135
Chapter 17 Getting to the Source: Choosing the Right Attribution Models	141
Chapter 18 Artificial Intelligence and Marketing Automation	148
Chapter 19 Pushing the Boundaries of Reality: AR and VR	154
Chapter 20 The Growth of Voice Commerce	160
Chapter 21 The Explosion of Vernacular Content	164
Appendix: Digital Marketing Jargon Busters	*171*

Book Outline

Upper Funnel: Building your brand and making your audience aware of who you are and what you have to offer.

- Setting your marketing objective
- Establishing a brand persona
- Making the transition from offline to online
- Laying the foundation of a strong digital presence
- How customers are changing
- Customer profiling and personalization of the customer journey

Middle Funnel: Earning your audiences' trust and imparting more knowledge on what your brand has to offer.

Part I: Owned media

- Improving findability with SEO and content
- UX – the key to success
- Storytelling via videos
- Social media strategy

Part II: Paid media

- Choosing the right platforms
- Influencer Marketing

Lower Funnel: Going the extra mile to convert potential customers into a loyal customer, and driving ROI to meet your goals.

- Intent-based targeting
- The boon of Market Place and OTT

Measurement and Driving Business Results

- Measuring results through digital marketing
- Online-offline integration
- Attribution Models

The Future of Digital

- AI and Marketing Automation
- VR
- Voice commerce
- Multi-lingual

Appendix

- Jargon Busters

Introduction

Every year, the bone-dry grasslands of the Serengeti are the centre for one of the most incredible spectacles of all time. Millions of wildebeest and zebras wade their way through the savannahs, barely visible through the storm of dust that they kick up. Their 800 kilometre-long journey has only one purpose: to escape the drought-stricken, parched lands of Tanzania in search of lush green pastures in the Masai Mara. This awe-striking event happens like clockwork, every year for the last thousands of years. Throughout the long history of our planet, this remains one of the greatest migratory events to ever occur.

Moving from the natural to the human world, an even greater migration has been happening over the last two decades. With growing momentum, 59% of the human population (around 4.5 billion people) have 'migrated' to the internet. They have replaced their hand-written letters with hurriedly-typed text messages, dinners around the table with binge-watching sessions in front of a laptop and trips to the local grocery store with a single click on a mobile app. But the internet has spawned more than just a behavioural change in its disciples. The almost superhuman ability to gain any information, product or service needed at the click of a button, has brought about a sea change in the very personalities, motivations and needs of every single person holding a mobile phone in the palm of their hands.

While landscapes and consumers themselves have undergone a complete metamorphosis, one of the fundamental diktats of advertising remains unchanged: a brand must go where its consumers are. And today, consumers are more likely to see an ad while scrolling through their feed rather than flipping through a newspaper, hear about a brand from a complete stranger on the internet than a close confidante and learn about a product while actively searching for information online than by reading the back of the box.

In this fast-evolving landscape, how do brands continue to grow and reach their audience?

Maybe the answer to this question lies where we first began: in the Serengeti. Our uber high-tech lives might seem worlds away from the savannah, but there are surprising similarities between the manmade and natural worlds. For instance, building a tribe, establishing dominance and leaving a legacy are equally important for a brand as they are for a new male lion taking over a pride. And like the changing seasons of the grasslands, digital marketing is marked with trends which come and go, but the underlying principles remain constant. So, let's leave the four walls and countless screens that mark our lives behind and instead go on a safari. Let's re-learn the fundamental concepts of digital marketing through a new lens: through the eyes of the multitude of creatures that call the savannah home.

On this journey, we will delve deep into the very essence of branding and marry traditional concepts of marketing with tenets that are adapted for the digital age. We will understand the modern consumer in their entirety, uncovering their challenges, wants and aspirations. Together, we will master the art of storytelling on new platforms, enhance a consumer's experience with a brand's online assets and identify proven strategies to boost online sales.

The Great Internet Migration of the 21st century is far from over. New users are coming online by the second, and in India, this change is happening at lightning speed.

Are you ready to ride this wave?

Upper Funnel: Building Your Brand Online

We've heard the word 'brand' tossed around a thousand times, but what really is at the crux of a brand? How do you shape a strong online brand presence that has the power to trigger action and edge out competitors?

Chapter 1

The Rallying Cry for Your Herd: Setting Your Marketing Objective

When the tribe of the Masai Mara laid eyes on the vast expanse of flatlands around them, they coined it the 'Serengeti', which translates to 'endless plains'. The continuous churn of wildebeest herds through these lands appeared to indicate a never-ending expanse of lands. But this seemingly chaotic event is fuelled by one single purpose among the herd: to chase the rains and get to greener fields. This driving force dictates the entire lifecycle of every wildebeest, from their birth to their death.

A marketing objective is a similar phenomenon. Every subsequent section of your digital strategy will flow from what your main objective is. How do you set in place an evergreen objective that will guide your herd and withstand the passage of time?

There's a famous Chinese proverb that says, 'A journey of a thousand miles begins with a single step'. Where you choose to place that first step can determine whether you reach your destination or fumble along an unknown path and get lost. Explorers in search of new continents were well aware of this. They often spent years planning their sea route and mapping trade winds before even stepping a heeled boot onto a ship.

Modern-day marketers, much like ancient-day voyagers, need a clear compass and map to succeed. Without this clarity, a brand is very likely to get lost at sea, missed by no one and forgotten by all.

Seafaring metaphors aside, there is a clear reason why, before you start planning the next viral campaign, you need to take a step back and ask yourself the question, "Why?". Why does your product or service even exist? Why should anyone buy it? Why should they choose you over your competitors? Penning down the answers to these questions will give you the single guiding light you, your team and future teams will need: your marketing objective.

Metrics vs Mission

A marketing objective is the framework from which every single action taken by your organization will flow. It is a set of goals around which any strategy, whether it's your marketing calendar for the year, product innovations and even talent acquisition, will centre around. In a nutshell, the marketing objective is your brand's raison d'etre.

But before we get into the framework for creating a marketing objective, it's important to separate a good objective from a bad one.

A bad marketing objective is myopic, uses fancy jargon to cover up the fact that it doesn't really mean anything and is inflexible.

A good marketing objective, on the other hand, is far-reaching, simple for anyone to understand and is versatile enough to stand the test of time and inspire people.

Here's how a good and bad marketing objective can shape your brand.

Case #1

A liquid hand soap brand formulates a new marketing objective: Increase QoQ new customer acquisition by 20% in new and emerging urban markets by being the premium liquid soap brand.

This objective pushes the marketing team to increase sales, but doesn't push them to think outside the box or build a long-term innovative strategy. In keeping with it, the team churns out the same old ads touting the germ-killing benefits of their brand's soap. Perfectly harmless, but the only problem of course, is that their competitors are doing the exact same thing.

Will this brand strike a chord with their audience and carve out a niche in their psyche? Probably not.

Case #2

A new visionary marketing executive at the soap company throws out the old marketing objective and installs a radically different approach spearheaded by a new marketing marketing objective: Our soap safeguards the one thing that's most valuable to you: your health. With our soap, you can always be confident that you and your loved ones are in the best of hands.

Can such a change in marketing objective actually have a major impact on a brand's perception and performance? Absolutely.

In a not-so-different scenario, Lifebuoy, one of the oldest soap brands in India, overhauled its marketing objective along the same lines and launched one of the most memorable digital campaigns in India: Help a Child Reach 5. With over 19 million views on YouTube, the ad captures the feeling of pride, relief and gratitude a father feels when his child reaches the age of 5, a birthday almost 2 million children in India don't have the chance to celebrate because they fall victim to diseases that can be easily prevented by washing their hands with a good soap. In one fell swoop, the campaign, powered by the marketing objective, turned the brand from something often smirkingly referred to as the 'tatti soap' in the corridors of Hindustan Unilever, to a noble brand that protects the most vulnerable members of our society.

That is the power of a good marketing objective.

The Framework for Success

Philosophers and idealistic college students alike have spent many years pondering what the meaning of life truly is and have come up empty-handed. Fortunately for us marketers, it's much easier to establish a concrete reason for a brand's existence than it is for our own.

The answers to these three questions, and a little soul searching, will help you formulate a marketing objective for the ages.

Question #1 Why are You Here?

This is the most fundamental question for any brand's existence, but often the most difficult to answer. Usually, when trying to pen an answer, it might be useful to approach it from the reverse angle: what would happen if your brand did not exist? Would consumers lack a sustainable alternative that could positively impact the environment? Would consumers miss out on an opportunity to own a premium product at an affordable price? Would consumers be robbed of a chance to experience a completely innovative product that can simplify their life?

The answer to this question trims out the extraneous facets of your brand and drills down into the main reason why it exists. Ultimately, the answer to your 'why', will become the core around which your future marketing communications and campaigns centre.

Of course, if you can't think of any change that would happen in a world where your brand doesn't exist, then you might have a larger problem on your hands.

Question #2 Who are You Here for?

The 'who' of your marketing objective seeks to pinpoint your target audience. The key word here is 'target'. Your campaigns need to be shaped by targeted communications rather than by casting the net far and wide and hoping for the best. Knowing exactly who you are speaking to will help you uncover exactly what pain points you are seeking to address and the right things to say if you want to resonate with consumers.

All too often, while defining their target audience, brands fall into the trap of using unimaginative, black and white demographic details. You might, for instance, define your shampoo brand's target audience as 'Women in the age group of 25–40, residing in metro cities, middle to upper income group'. This might tell you the targeting parameters to set for your ads, but it won't tell you what to communicate in them.

Psychographic details go beyond just the objective details of your audience and drill down into what motivates them, their needs and aspirations, pain points and struggles. Understanding the answers to these questions will help you formulate a marketing objective that really speaks *to* a consumer rather than *at* them.

Ever noticed that most mid-segment detergent brands centre around a mother sending her child to school in a sparkling white uniform and proudly looking on as the child wins awards and aces exams? Numerous focus groups to uncover psychographic insights uncovered that the greatest priority for lower-middle class parents is to ensure that they give their child every opportunity to create a better future for themselves. Detergent brands then used this insight to cater to the aspirational values of mid-segment consumers. Had they stuck to pure demographic data alone, they would have been unable to produce ads half as compelling.

When pinpointing the target audience and psychographic details of your consumers, there's one pitfall that marketers should consciously avoid: personal bias. It can be too tempting to project your own likes and dislikes onto your target audience. Doing so would not only be inaccurate, but potentially devastating for your brand.

Question #3 What is Your Brand Promise?

The final question, and the clinching argument, is what does your brand promise to do. A brand promise is something you guarantee your consumers will experience once they purchase your product. Let's be clear, customers never purchase a product out of any sense of magnanimity, they purchase it because they want something from it. The final factor that will determine whether they add your product to their cart or a competitor's is the extent to which they believe your product will fulfill their requirement.

The brand promise differs from your brand's mission and vision statement in that it speaks from a consumer's perspective. It's not so much about what your brand seeks to accomplish, but about what experience consumers will have once they try your product or service. So while your brand's mission statement might be about becoming the number one go-to brand among your target audience, your brand's promise will be about helping your consumers feel empowered and confident once they use your product.

The tricky part here is that what a consumer is looking for in your brand isn't always a clear, tangible benefit. It can be something completely intangible, or a perceived benefit. For instance, in the example of the detergent brands, mothers weren't always looking for the product that got stains out the best. They were looking for the product that would give their child a leg up in life.

So how do you uncover the innermost wants of your audience, desires that they might not even know they have? This can only come through in-depth consumer research; something that we will delve into in Part II.

With these parameters in place, you will be able to formulate a marketing objective that can become the guiding force for your company for many years to come. But while a marketing objective sets the stage for all your marketing activities, the real star of the show is the brand itself. Creating a brand that has the power to inspire and motivate consumers is what will ultimately deliver results. While this has long been understood to be the case in offline advertising, many digital marketers tend to forego this critical step. What marketers need to remember is that higher ad spends do not guarantee higher interest levels among consumers. That is almost wholly determined by how much consumers identify with your brand and believe in it.

In the next chapter, we will answer the most fundamental question: what *is* a brand anyway? And how do you build one for the digital age?

CHAPTER 2

The Making of a Main Attraction: Establishing a Brand Persona

The Masai Mara is home to around 90 species of animals and 500 species of birds; each beautiful and unique in their own right. But ask any tourist what animals they're most excited to see and the answer is invariably, 'The Big 5'. This elite group (lion, leopard, elephant, black rhino and African buffalo) has carved a name for itself that attracts wildlife-enthusiasts from across the world. In other words, these animals have built a 'brand'.

A strong brand is almost like a person. It has a set of traits and principles that are unique to it and become its calling card. Take a leaf out of the Big 5 and build a brand that has the power to attract your audiences and stand out from the crowd.

What makes a consumer pick your product off the shelf? What makes them order food from you when they are hungry? What makes them walk into your store as soon as they need something?

'Branding' as a concept has existed for many centuries; right from the time, rival merchants vied with each other to attract a group of consumers. The internet, however, only entered the public consciousness as recently as 1991. Within a blink of an eye, it has transformed into the world's biggest melting pot of cultures, people, ideas and, of course, businesses. The internet has flattened every geographical divide and has brought people closer than ever before. A brand's competitors aren't just confined to their immediate geographical location; they now span across the world. In this oversaturated market, it has become even more important for brands to establish a personality for themselves that can help distinguish them from the hundreds, sometimes thousands, of other brands competing to attract the attention of consumers.

Branding in the digital space has one fundamental difference from branding in the pre-internet era: communication is now two-way.

BRANDING THEN

I'm going to tell my audience what my brand stands for

BRANDING NOW

My audience is going to tell me what they think of my brand and I'm going to try to make their experience with it positive

---

Let's take a trip back in time to 1980s India. The television had just started making an entry into people's homes and the internet as a concept didn't even exist. A family might encounter an advertisement for a new brand of coffee powder in the newspaper, in billboards outside their homes and, if they belonged to a more affluent class, on a television ad. Motivated by this exposure, they decide to purchase the brand, but find it to be far from as rich and aromatic as it was marketed to be. The disgruntled family members might tell their neighbours or immediate family, but apart from this, their power to do anything else would be extremely limited.

Fast forward to the present day and the family has no dearth of options to vent out their frustrations on the coffee brand. They could write on the brand's social media platforms, put up a post on their own profiles or directly message the brand. The coffee brand, in turn, would be alarmed by the impact that these negative comments could have on their sales. In an effort to mollify the consumers and change their perception of the brand, they might send them free samples, give them a refund on their purchase or even take their feedback to heart and improve their product

In this scenario, the guardians of a brand's image are not just a corporate team in a glass office, it is the public. Brands need to adapt their branding strategies to suit this shift from

'broadcast' to 'conversation'.

The Cola Conundrum

Why have Coca-Cola and Pepsi spawned such intense rivalry between those consumers who prefer one over the other? Is it that one group likes red more while the other loves blue? Probably not. Is it because one likes the brand ambassador of Coca-Cola while the other prefers Pepsi's? Also unlikely since the brand ambassadors of the two keep changing. Is it because one group likes the taste of Coca-Cola while the other group likes the sweetness of Pepsi? Not likely since in one experiment, while participants preferred the taste of Pepsi, they still self-identified as die-hard Coke fans.

The real answer is far simpler, but in many ways, more complicated. The two groups simply align themselves with what each brand stands for.

This phenomenon is far from limited to just Pepsi vs. Coke. Consumers everywhere make purchase decisions based on what the brand stands for, or what they perceive the brand to stand for. This begs the question: what *is* a brand?

Many companies tend to agonize over the visual aspect of a brand: its logo, the brand colours, the tagline, etc. But the true essence of a brand is completely intangible. Call it an X-factor, a certain je ne sais quoi, something you can't quite put your finger on; a 'brand' is more than just the sum of its parts. A brand is a living, breathing, *person*.

In the same way that people judge our personality by their interactions with us, what other people have said about us and by our actions, your consumers are building their perception of your brand. Essentially, your brand's personality is the sum of every touchpoint your consumers have with it. As your brand steps into the digital world, these touchpoints will also begin to include online interactions as well. Each of these independent interactions morph together to create something more powerful than any company's mission statement can: a *brand*.

Brand Gestalt

Back in the early twentieth century, a group of German and Austrian psychologists discovered that human beings gravitate towards complete patterns, shapes or forms. Even if a pattern is made up of separate parts, they can connect the dots in their minds and understand what the pattern actually represents. This pattern is why human beings see this diagram as a triangle, rather than three circles with missing sectors.

How does this psychological theory apply to brands? Well, think of it this way. Your consumers rarely, if ever, have only one single interaction with your brand. Usually, a consumer might come across an Instagram ad for your brand while scrolling through their phone, watch a television commercial for it while eating their breakfast, pass a billboard advertising your product on the way to work, see ads for it on websites that they are browsing through and maybe even receive direct emails promoting the product. When they decide to purchase your product, they will either interact with your website or look at your store display and packaging. Even after they use your product, they might need to get in touch with customer support if they have any questions.

Each of these individual, independent interactions creates a composite brand perception in the minds of your customers. If each touchpoint is consistent in its communication, then consumers develop a strong image of your brand, one that matches what you want them to perceive. If, on the other hand, your communication is disjointed, then your customers will fail to develop a cohesive perception of your brand and will therefore, also fail to develop an emotional connection with it.

Finding Your Brand Voice

Every person has a fundamental character that comes out in the way they speak, their actions, their aspirations, likes, dislikes and more. When we get to know a person, we start understanding their character and more or less come to expect certain things from them. This is why it's so jarring when a person does something 'out of character'.

Successful brands operate in more or less the same way. They adopt a personality and make sure that all of their brand communication, whether verbal or visual, falls in line with it.

While there are innumerable brands out there in the world, research has shown that almost every brand falls into one of twelve specific brand personality types. These 12 brand archetypes are an extension of Carl Jung's theory on personality archetypes. The best way to start building a strong brand is to first identify which of the 12 personas your brand best identifies with.

1. The Creator

What it is: Creators love out-of-the-box thinking and are always in search of something newer and better.

Brand promise: To surpass the limits of one's imagination to deliver outstandingly innovative products or services that have the power to amaze and inspire.

Weakness: The relentless pursuit for perfection can prevent Creators from slowing down and focusing on the present. Creator brands also continually fear about not being *the* most innovative product in the market and of being overshadowed.

Messaging: Stresses individuality and freedom of expression.

Brand colours: Bright yellows, reds and pinks signify the vibrancy of Creator brands

Examples of Creators: Apple and Lego

2. The Innocent

What it is: Just as the name implies, the Innocent are pure, optimistic, down-to-earth and loving. They seek simplicity over complexity and connections over conflicts.

Brand promise: Make the world a happier place by always looking for the good in people and situations.

Weakness: The Innocent's determination to always believe the best can come across as gullible, naive or simplistic. Since these brands consciously steer clear of edgy messaging, they can also sometimes run the risk of appearing bland.

Messaging: Harkens back to the golden days, when things were simple and joyful. Many ads revolve around nostalgic trips down memory lane.

Brand colours: Pastel mauves, pinks and greens signify the purity of the Innocent.

Examples of Innocent brands: Dove and Coca Cola

3. The Rebel

What it is: The Rebel wants to overthrow the status quo. Rebel brands question the legitimacy of things that are often taken for granted and want to bring about a change.

Brand promise: Bring about a revolution by breaking the rules and doing away with old, obsolete ideas.

Weakness: The Rebel's stirring ideas can sometimes toe the line of encouraging anti-social or illegal activity.

Messaging: Speaks directly to those who feel like an outcast from mainstream society by encouraging them to celebrate their uniqueness and bringing them together as a tribe.

Brand colours: Moody colours like black, maroon and dark blue best reflect the Rebel brand personality.

Examples of Rebel Brands: MTV and Harley Davidson

Examples of Sage brands: Discovery channel, Google, CNN

4. The Everyman

What it is: The Everyman openly shuns all efforts at pretentiousness, preferring to be a genuine, wholesome and family-oriented brand.

Brand promise: Wholeheartedly accept everyone into a big happy family.

Weakness: The Everyman's constant efforts to please everyone can often result in their own identity becoming diluted.

Messaging: Practical and down-to-earth communication that reinforces the inherent self-worth of every individual.

Brand colours: Solid colours like dark blue and ochre communicate the stability of Everyman brands.

Examples of Everyman Brands: TATA, Ford

5. The Sage

What is it: The Sage brand persona is all-knowing, deeply intellectual and keen to pass on their knowledge to educate consumers

Brand promise: Provide the best-in-class experience to consumers, one that is based on and validated by meticulous research.

Weakness: The overly analytical nature of The Sage can sometimes make it seem like a brand that is hesitant to take action.

Messaging: The Sage takes pride in its knowledge, so all communication is in highly-sophisticated language and is aimed at encouraging consumers to learn.

Brand colours: Strong but soothing colours like dusty rose and peacock blue best suit Sage brands.

6. The Explorer

What it is: The Explorer is constantly on a quest to self-actualization, venturing into the unknown and setting a path for themselves.

Brand promise: To help consumers discover their true selves by encouraging them to travel down the unbeaten path.

Weakness: The Explorer's need for new experiences can sometimes come off as an unwillingness to commit.

Messaging: Encourage users to take risk through imagery of the great outdoors, rugged paths and unknown territories.

Brand colours: Earth tones like forest green and brown bring out the outdoorsiness of The Explorer.

Examples of Explorer brands: Thar, National Geographic

7. The Entertainer

What it is: The Entertainer's primary mission is to make people laugh, have a wonderful time and forget about all their worries.

Brand promise: To make consumers feel happy and cheerful by using humour and wit to lighten the mood.

Weakness: The Entertainer can sometimes come across as too frivolous.

Messaging: Enthusiastic and energetic, Entertainer brands are never scared to be 'in-your-face' with their messaging.

Brand colours: Fun colours like sunshine yellow, bubblegum pink and bright purple evoke the sense of irreverence that Entertainer brands are known for.

Examples of Entertainer brands: Snickers, 7UP

8. The Seducer

What it is: The Seducer values love and intimacy above all else. However, it's important to make the distinction that the intimacy isn't always romantic in nature; it could be closeness between friends, families and even with oneself.

Brand promise: Seducer brands want to make each one of their consumers feel special, valued and loved.

Weakness: Brands should be careful to never cross the line between romantic and sleazy.

Messaging: The Seducer uses suggestive messages and imagery to capture a consumer's attention, but the core message is always about finding a connection and feeling loved.

Brand colours: Romantic colours like red, pink and deep purple symbolize the sultry persona of Seducer brands.

Examples of Seducer brands: Slice, Magnum

9. The Magician

What it is: For Magician brands, there is no such thing as impossible. These brands strive to bring their imagination to life, breaking every barrier in their way.

Brand promise: To constantly amaze and delight you by turning your wildest dreams into reality

Weakness: Magician brands can sometimes appear overly restless and manipulative.

Messaging: Create a sense of wonder and amazement and encourage consumers to stretch the limit of their imagination.

Brand colours: Violet and sooty black embody the aura of m mysticism that Magician brands create.

Example of Magician brands: Tesla, Disney

10. The Hero

What it is: The Hero is courageous and daring, always believing that people have more potential than they believe they do.

Brand promise: To challenge your limits and empower you to achieve things you might not have thought yourself capable of.

Weakness: The motivational attitude of Hero brands can sometimes appear to be too pushy and demanding.

Messaging: The Hero is your greatest cheerleader, sending out motivational messages and encouraging people to believe in themselves.

Brand colours: Colours traditionally associated with superheroes, such as true blues and royal reds are often used by Hero brands.

Examples of Hero brands: Nike, Whisper

11. The Ruler

What it is: The Rules symbolizes power and leadership; they are industry leaders and they take pride in that fact.

Brand promise: These brands impart a sense of control and leadership in their consumers.

Weakness: The Ruler's need for power can sometimes appear to be controlling and conceited.

Messaging: Validates a consumer's need for power, prestige and prosperity.

Brand colours: Regal plums and royal blues bring out the royalty of elite Ruler brands.

Examples of Ruler brands: IBM, Microsoft

12. The Caregiver

What it is: The Caregiver is nurturing and protective, wanting to offer the best possible experience to consumers.

Brand promise: To take care of all of your needs and make you feel safe and secure.

Weakness: Caregiver brands should make a conscious effort not to come across as a 'saviour' as this might be perceived as condescending.

Messaging: To protect you and all that you care about and to provide a safe and loving environment.

Brand colours: Pastel pinks and robin's egg blues bring out the nurturing attitude of Caregivers.

Examples of Caregiver brands: Johnson & Johnson, Pampers

Building a brand is a consistent and continuous labour of love. Setting your brand identity early on is critical because once your brand personality has been developed and established, it becomes very difficult to change it. People develop strong bonds with the brands they love; revamping the brand personality can come as a rude shock.

But while changing your brand personality drastically can have negative consequences, it is important to update certain facets of it to keep it relevant and fresh. One of the biggest overhauls to your brand image comes when you are planning to move from an offline presence to an online one. When done right, making this shift can help your brand create a splash and tap into a new market. When done wrong, it could result in two worst-case scenarios: either your online branding doesn't resonate with your online consumers or your efforts at refreshing your brand image alienate your offline consumers. In the next chapter, we will help give your brand a digital makeover and take the online world by storm.

CHAPTER 3

The Leap of Faith: Moving from Offline to Online

While the Great Migration is indeed a sight to behold, like all things with nature, it is just as brutal as it is beautiful. Thousands of animals attempting to cross the rivers cutting through the plains never make it to the other side. The unforgiving jaws of crocodiles lying in wait within the murky depths of the water are only too willing to snap up an animal that makes just one wrong step.

Crossing the river from the offline to the online world can be intimidating for brands who are yet to make the leap. One misstep and you could fail to create a splash among the wider audience available online. But building a strong online presence goes further than setting up a website and creating a Facebook page. It requires you to take cognizance of your consumer's entire journey through the offline and online world.

Making a major life change is never easy. There are bound to be fumbles, major adjustments and miscalculations along the way. The same holds true when you are moving a brand that has largely been exclusively offline and bringing it into the expansive world of the internet. With the internet having been around for so long, it's unlikely that your brand will have absolutely no internet presence. At the very least, you might have a functioning website and a few social media handles. But at the crux of a successful brand relocation is not migration, but adaptability. It's not simply adding a few online assets and calling it a day, but really leveraging the online space to its fullest potential. This task is something that even many of the biggest offline players fail to implement.

What is at Stake Here?

A study by Boston Consulting Group and Nielsen estimated that by 2020, India's online consumer spending would blow up to $100 billion. Much of this spending would be driven by younger audiences who have become well-versed in the online space and are comfortable making transactions on it. Everything from essential items like groceries to big-ticket items like consumer durables and electronics will be bought online in the near future.

The need for a digital-first strategy is also just as relevant in sectors like real estate and automobiles, industries where purchases still happen largely offline and will, in all likelihood, continue to do so. This is because while the final purchase might happen offline, each of the steps leading up to it has moved online. Unless they have come into a major inheritance, no one simply walks into a dealership and purchases a car on a whim. There is almost always weeks, or even months, of online research, trawling through reviews and booking a site visit/test drive online before the final purchase decision is made.

Because of this, a holistic online presence is no longer a 'nice-to-have' feature; it's integral to your brand's future.

The Two Mistakes of Digitization

The road to digitizing your brand can be a bumpy one if you don't know the common pitfalls to steer clear off.

Mistake #1 You Simply Move Your Offline Communication Online

Have a successful TVC that grabbed eyeballs when it was broadcasted during primetime TV? It would make sense to move the same commercial online where it can enjoy the same success, right? Wrong.

Online advertising formats and communications are fundamentally different from the offline versions because consumers themselves approach these two mediums differently.

When online, most people are in a 'discovery mindset'. They want to learn about something specific and are looking for a resource that can provide them with the most credible information. There are two ways your brand can take advantage of this; you can either be the provider of that information or, if your brand is relevant to the search, your ads can be displayed on the search results page or the website that the user is scrolling through. Both of these methods have one very important distinction: they are engaging with a consumer, they are not interrupting them.

The 'one-to-many' approach characterized by most traditional forms of advertising simply does not work in the digital space. Consumers are not obliged to pay you any attention. Because of this, your online communication needs to be targeted, relevant and above all, useful.

Mistake #2 You Adopt a Drastically Different Brand Approach

On the other end of the spectrum are brands who agree that the online space needs a different strategy, but might take it to the other extreme. In this case, the brand can stray too far from its offline image and essentially split down the middle into two brands. The consequences of this are obvious; your consumers can be confused about the dissonance between the two avatars and end up failing to connect with both.

While adapting certain aspects of your brand image is vital to moving online, it's important to remember that the main pillars of your brand persona cannot completely morph into something else entirely. A caregiver brand, for instance, cannot switch to a rebel brand simply because it sees a larger potential for this segment online. This pitfall is commonly seen in large established offline brands that are trying to capture a younger audience online. Younger internet audiences can view the brand as out of touch while the conservative offline crowd can be put off by its new approach. At the end of the day, the brand fails to impress either group.

Think of your brand as akin to the Constitution. The Constitution of India is a living document that judicial authorities are free to interpret, but the core tenets are permanent and dissoluble. In the same way, your brand's stance on current issues, its vocabulary and even its typography can be updated, but it's core raison d'etre, it's marketing objective and its brand persona must remain constant.

The Changing Customer Journey

Consumers are highly unique individuals, each with their own personal history that has moulded their likes, dislikes, aspirations and fears. To club entire groups of them into one homogeneous category would undoubtedly be ineffective and inaccurate. But as diverse as they are, most consumers still go through the same broad phases when they are planning on purchasing a product. For decades, marketers have tried to decode this journey and align their marketing approach to cater to it. One of the most popular theories that emerged out of this was 'AIDA'.

The customer journey was thought to follow four predictable stages:

A for 'awareness'

I for 'interest'

D for 'desire'

A for 'action'

In the past, brand communications were supposed to influence the customer through this process until they bought the brand or product. It was, however, very difficult to directly attribute how, when and how many were being influenced, and how many would buy. At best, periodic consumer research would throw up opportunities that could be used to further this objective. In some cases, incentivized promotions would spur action if latent demand was identified.

Moving Away From AIDA

The AIDA approach was effective for a long time, but there is one problem with it: AIDA was first developed in 1898. The customer journey that took place over a century ago is drastically different from the one that takes place today. Today's tech-savvy customers make their purchase decisions in a completely new environment, one where all the information in the world is accessible through a small device in their pocket, where advertisements are more ubiquitous than ever before and where a far greater number of brands are vying for their wallet.

The greatest change in the customer journey is that it is no longer linear. Traditionally, a customer would take note of a certain brand, be seduced by its advertisements and ultimately, take action and purchase it. Today, however, a customer can add a product to cart, abandon it, research a lot more on it, hear positive reviews about it from others and then eventually go back and purchase it. The key point to note here is that for most customers these days, research plays a vital role in their decision making process. Customers are more aware of the tricks that marketers have up their sleeves and are unwilling to accept a brand's communication at face value.

AIDA is simply not equipped to cater to this leapfrogging, well-informed and oftentimes cynical customer.

Adaptation of AIDA

As measurement methods for media and research became more sophisticated, the AIDA process was further refined into the marketing funnel:

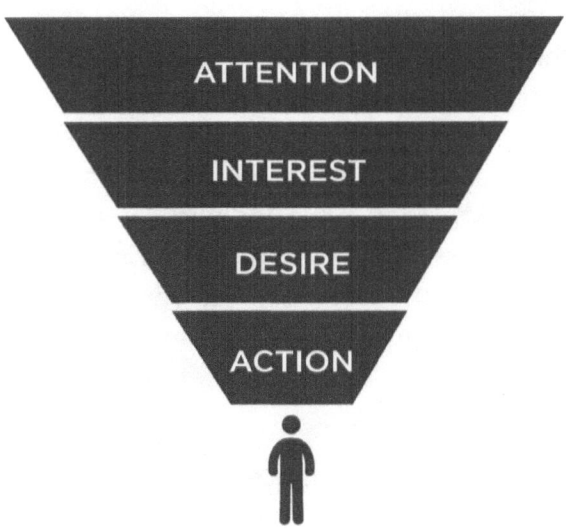

What this essentially did was place the AIDA concept into a process diagram using a funnel to visually depict the importance of spreading awareness to as many people as possible and catching their attention (The wide top of the funnel); moving some of them into the consideration stage by building up their interest and desire for the product (Middle of the funnel) and moving some of these into the conversion stage by getting them to act (Bottom of the funnel). Some depictions also show a lower level of the funnel depicting loyalty among some of those who bought the product. However, it still was a challenge to manage & monitor this process using offline broadcast media.

The Digital Funnel

The digital funnel takes into account the new stages of the customer's journey and places greater emphasis on engagement over pure action. For the modern marketer, a fully-engaged customer is just as important as one who has made a purchase. But apart from the adapted customer journey, a digital funnel has one clear distinction from older models: it is completely trackable right down to the last detail.

The Internet and digital platforms have made managing & monitoring the process of the funnel possible because it gives you complete control and visibility into each customer's journey. It enables accurate, informed targeting of individuals, remarketing to them if they have engaged with previous ads, providing them with the information they were looking for on the product, and so on. Their interests, preferences and behaviour can also be understood through the analytics on various platforms such as Google, Facebook, Instagram, YouTube etc. In this way, you're not just guiding a customer through the funnel, but you're actually *managing* their whole journey.

The digital funnel also reduces process time. In the offline marketing funnel, this took a very long time because people respond to broadcast messaging very slowly over time. research took time to estimate where consumers were because it was field surveys that were collated. There was no real content solution for those in the consideration phase except very informative ads or advertorials. So it was hit or miss, spray and pray over time

The digital funnel, because we can now manage the process, telescopes time so that a brand's marketing efforts with a full-funnel approach is able to convert prospects into customers faster than ever before

In light of this, the objective of shifting a brand from offline to online might better be worded as *integrating* offline and online. Both your offline and online activities cannot operate in silos because they are essentially two sides of the same consumer's decision making journey.

Most brands when moving to digital for the first time tend to focus only on the bottom of the funnel. They use traditional media to create awareness and digital platforms only to drive purchases or enquiries. This approach is not only ineffective, but it can also cause you serious loss in revenue through increased cost-per-acquisitions.

Adapting Brand Communication to the Online Sphere

With changing customer journeys, the nature of brand communications must also change when shifting from offline to online communication. Traditional marketing largely relied on *unified messages* broadcast on different mediums such as TV, newspapers, magazines, billboards & radio to relentlessly hammer home the brand's promise.

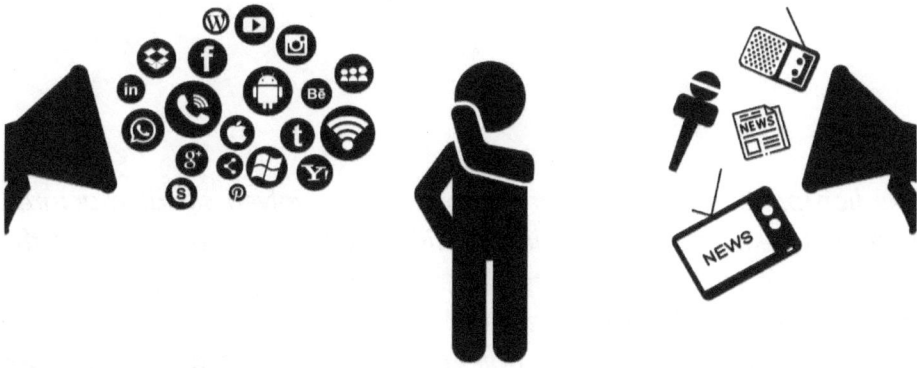

This is not how it works in digital marketing, in fact, it is the very opposite. A successful digital communication strategy involves diverse pieces of content spread across various platforms. The ultimate goal is that no matter what platform the customer is active on, or what type of content related to your brand they are interested in, your brand is visible and engaging. The brand's *value proposition* remains constant, but the communications across platforms vary widely depending on context and use case.

The efficacy of your communication strategy will depend upon how many platforms you are visible on and how your communication adapts to each of these. In the next chapter, we will be constructing a blueprint for your online presence to ensure that your brand is visible no matter where your consumers are.

CHAPTER 4

Demarcating Your Territory: The Foundation of a Strong Digital Presence

The lion pride is one of nature's most highly-evolved social structures. With a majestic male at its helm and fierce lionesses ready to attack, the pride will go to any lengths to defend their clear-cut territory. As they should. The pride chooses its territory based on the abundance of prey in the area, proximity to watering holes and enough cover to rear baby cubs before they're ready to step out onto the flat plains. These assets are vital to the continued survival of the pride and must be defended at all costs.

Brands also work within a clearly demarcated territory with clear assets. Setting up a physical footprint is easy enough. You lease out a space, put out a few billboards and everyone knows where to find you. But how do you carve out a strong presence on the intangible world wide web?

Before you carve out a presence in your consumer's mind, you need to first establish a presence in their physical realm of consciousness. In the recent past, this presence was mostly created through traditional channels. Brands would purchase TV spots on channels their customers watched, place billboards in their neighbourhoods and of course, set up an actual store in areas where their audience was concentrated. When consumer exposure was so clearly defined, this practice was relatively straightforward.

Now, of course, the main arena of consumer awareness has shifted to the online space. Unlike in traditional forms of advertising, online spaces are less tangible. The internet is simultaneously everywhere and yet nowhere. In this world, how do you still create a strong presence and get in front of your consumer?

The Power of Omnipresence

To reach your online audience, you need to be present on every channel, platform and medium they are on. But this goes beyond just creating profiles on these websites, it involves tweaking your own communication to suit the interests and preferences of your consumers based on each platform. They might, for instance look up a specific need on Google, scroll through social media in their break, pose a question on a community forum and look up reviews for a specific product. Your brand needs to be front and centre at each one of these touchpoints.

Creating powerful online assets for your brand is crucial if you want to reach out to these customers. Online advertisements can create interest and awareness in your product, but online *assets* will help build a longstanding relationship with customers and project your brand values.

While the exact online assets to create can vary from each sector and brand, in general, there is a reliable blueprint of assets you should build and improve upon.

1. Website

A website is quite possibly the most important digital asset you can have. It's a culmination of all your brand, social, content and SEO strategies neatly packaged in one place. For example, your social media posts might direct users to your website for more information, your content will have to be hosted on your website and all your SEO techniques will be geared towards increasing visibility of your website.

In the realm of the world wide web, your website is your brand's virtual address. Like a physical store, it can display your products, offer assistance and help users make a purchase. But unlike an offline store, it can also demonstrate your expertise, provide informative content to engage users who might not be ready to make a purchase and provide multiple different calls to action (such as newsletter sign ups and downloads).

For your website to achieve these goals, it needs to tick these critical boxes:

- **Branding:** Your website is possibly the most important aspect of your brand image. To deliver a cohesive experience to your user, make sure that your brand tonality and aesthetics conform to the brand guidelines set out.
- **Mobile responsiveness:** With most internet users in India circumventing the desktop phase completely and coming online through their mobile phones, your website should be adapted to the small screen.
- **Speed:** Most Indian internet users access the internet through 3G or 2G mobile connections. With a slow website loading speed, you might see a greater number of drop offs and fewer conversions.
- **Discoverability:** Even the most stunning website is of no use if no one is able to find it. Optimization of content with focus keywords, technical SEO fixes and link building to the website are essential to improve organic visibility of your website for relevant searches.

2. Social Media

Social Media is undoubtedly the best way to continuously engage with your target audience through relevant and impactful campaigns. While there are a plethora of social media platforms available and the exact mix will depend upon your brand's segment, the Big Three are largely recognized as the basic platforms every brand should be active on:

- **Facebook:** Over 310 million Indians actively use Facebook, spanning across demographics like age and gender. Regardless of which industry you belong to, you can bet that your audience is on Facebook. Apart from running successful campaigns, Facebook can also be used as a platform to support your customer service. Many users prefer reaching out to brands through the Messenger option, so making use of this feature can significantly improve your customer service capabilities.

- **Instagram:** Instagram is one of the most powerful ways to drive engagement among your users; one study discovered that Instagram offers 58 times more engagement per user compared to Facebook and 150 times higher engagement per user compared to Twitter. Instagram also offers higher conversion rates than most other platforms, specifically for brands in the fashion, e-commerce and F&B space.

- **LinkedIn:** While LinkedIn offers advantages to companies across sectors, it's especially beneficial to B2B companies. While the audience on LinkedIn tends to be smaller, they are highly qualified and are coming to the platform for specific purposes, whether it's to increase their knowledge, network with influential peers or improve their career. B2B companies can use this to their advantage by demonstrating their thought leadership and professional solutions on this platform.

3. Quora

Quora is an often overlooked and criminally under-utilized platform by most brands. This is the most popular question and answer website in the world, with topics ranging from healthcare and beauty to technology and business. Essentially, no matter what area your business operates in, you can be sure that a user has queries about it on Quora.

But with the already active community more than willing to offer their expert advice to every question, why does your brand need to hop on the bandwagon? The ultimate goal of any product innovation is to address a clear need that your customers have. Quora is the platform where the most openly express that need. This is why the platform offers the perfect opportunity to address a user's query, educate them and start cultivating trust in your brand.

Like with most platforms, there's a wrong way to use Quora and a right way. The wrong way to use Quora is to write lacklustre responses and use it primarily as a way to post links back to your website. This practice, commonly called 'astroturfing' isn't just likely to get you banned from the platform, but also creates suspicion among users who start to view your brand as opportunistic and self-motivated. The right way to use Quora is to provide the most detailed and accurate response to a user's question and mention your brand only when absolutely necessary. This can help you build a large following and establish you as a leader in the space.

4. Local SEO Listings

For many segments like auto, real estate and retail, digital platforms are not the primary sales channels. While some purchases might happen online, digital marketing is mostly used to create awareness and drive consumers to making an offline purchase. Even when this is the case, a strong online presence is essential to inform users of where you are located and how they can reach there. Local SEO listings, commonly known as GMB (Google My Business) listings are an informative SERP feature that provides a user with details of your offline presence. These details include:

- Your address with a map location
- Opening and closing hours
- Customer reviews

- Contact details
- Pictures of your store
- Website address
- Any posts from your website that you may want to highlight

Monitoring and optimizing your local listing is important because you want your customers to see your verified listing and visit your store. In many cases, when listings are not updated or optimized, a competitor listing or duplicate listing can take over and steal your spot. In such an event, a consumer might be directed to a competitor store or be provided with the wrong details.

These foundational elements of a digital presence will ensure that you have a strong base from where you can launch a full-fledged and effective online marketing strategy.

CHAPTER 5

Adaptation and Evolution: The Changing Consumer

If you were to stand in the middle of the Masai Mara, you'd be tempted to believe that these extensive grasslands were untouched and free from human intervention. But the increasing advancements of human settlements around the periphery of the sanctuary and increased illegal grazing of domestic cattle in wild territory tell a different story. These changes have led to higher competition for resources and have forced wild grazers like gazelle and wildebeest to adapt their grazing patterns.

Nothing is ever constant and as marketers, we need to understand and adapt to the changing market. The simple truth is that consumers today are shaped by different experiences and have different worldviews from consumers at a time when most marketing theories were formulated.

Marketers have always studied consumer behaviour to understand how to appeal to them successfully. This understanding of behavior is what led to the development of the AIDA process, followed by the Marketing Funnel. Marketers sought to understand the process of decision making that drove behaviours depending on which part of the process the consumer was in.

Before the Internet, consumer behaviour was shaped by the influences they came under over the course of each day by brand messages beamed at them through diverse media. This resulted in 'media mapping' of the targeted consumer from morning to night – tracking them through their media consumption and exposure through the day. Typically, this was the newspaper in the morning, followed by radio in the car, and billboards they drove by to the office. In the evening it was again the car radio, billboards & lighted neons they passed, 'Out of Home' media if they stopped to shop (OOH), and finally prime time news & soaps later in the night. This was simpler as one could *predict* what media they were exposed to by the time of day and the activity they were performing.

Where they were in the marketing funnel depended on which messages had registered and were being acted upon. A print ad for a car, for example, may have triggered some level of interest in a person who needed to change his/her car for something bigger as the family grew. This interest may have been reinforced by a billboard display of the car on the way to work. A radio jingle on the delights of driving that car may have caught their ear on the way home. And, finally, a compelling television commercial may have held their attention before their favourite soap on TV. Mind you, it was highly unlikely that all this happened on the same day!

The exposure would have cascaded across time based on the media plan for the car launch: the initial launch burst on print & TV over a month or two, followed by radio for sustained exposure and billboards as a reminder & reinforcement of the message. This actual schedule could have been over 4 to 6 months as offline media is a very high investment proposition. Through the whole process, the target consumer was a passive receiver of the marketing message, influenced over time by what was called 'Opportunity to See', or OTS in media planning terms. The more OTS you could afford over time, the more likely you were to influence the prospect from awareness to consideration for them to finally seek more information.

After months of sustained exposure & reinforcement, the prospect may visit a dealership to collect more information, view the car, look at the models & pricing options as well as do the same for other cars in his/her consideration set. This is when you knew for sure that they were in the consideration phase of the funnel! Once they had distilled the information, spoken to relatives, friends or colleagues, they would narrow it down to a brand or two based on their desired criteria and the options offered. It is only then that they would move into the next phase of the funnel and visit the dealerships of the two brands under consideration to make a final decision.

Conversion would only take place based on their actual experience at the dealership. This would involve how they experienced the service of the person attending to them, the perceived benefits of the model, the price negotiated and whether they were offered a price reduction or a value add, and most importantly, the test drive and their actual experience of the brand in question. If the drive confirmed the impression they had formed up to then by all the exposure to the brand, conversion took place after the final negotiations, and they eventually drove the car home. And the process from start to finish may have taken 4 to 6 months.

All this has changed dramatically after the advent of the Internet and the various applications online that have become a part of our daily lives. These new set of influences have shaped modern-day consumers in critical ways.

Always-on Media

Today, consumption of media is constant, and initiated by the consumer throughout the day. So it is no longer largely determined by time of day. For example, one may read the news (on a newspaper's site)online many times during the day, or watch the news periodically on news channel's sites. The consumer is also not restricted to one paper or channel any longer, but reads or watches many sites based on who has the latest news or live coverage. Billboards, radio & OOH still play a role, but increasingly do not have the time-determined attention they commanded earlier because of the access to the smartphone. Consumers also initiate when they interact with which platform or application so that they are in control and not dependent on program or delivery schedules.

Always Engaged

Given that consumers initiate access increasingly on their smartphones, to either the media applications or other sites such as Facebook, Instagram, LinkedIn etc., they are engaged with these platforms as active participants instead of passive recipients of news or information. They comment, discuss, like and share articles, videos & posts that interest them with their network, whether it is a news article, news video clip, articles on diverse other topics, posts by brands, brand videos that caught their interest or any other content. Or, they create their own posts, commentaries, articles, pictures or videos and share them on facebook, LinkedIn, YouTube or TikTok or other platforms. So they are not only active participants online, they are also publishers!

The Discovery Mindset

Today, due to the vast amount of information available at their fingertips, consumers have developed what is called 'the discovery mindset'. The habit of searching online for whatever they feel they need or want, whether it is information on a place, person, product or brand, the best route to a destination, the best places to eat nearby or the weather. They are also more open to consuming content in any form that interests them, which is why videos on Facebook start as you scroll. If it interests them, they will watch it. They are also open to content that informs them about friends, family, public figures, brands, places or just about anything else. So they consume more content per day on more subjects than in the past. This means they are receptive to receiving brand messages or content that is presented in an interesting manner to them.

The Rise of the Smartphone

It is mind boggling that a smartphone today is packed with more processing power and capabilities than computers were decades ago. Add to that their affordability, and you have the rise of the smartphone as the primary device on which most people spend their time online. In fact, out of the over 700 million Internet users in India, 500 million are smartphone users. For the vast majority, the smartphone is their primary, if not their only device, for accessing the Internet. In this sense, India's journey to coming online has taken a completely different trajectory than most developed countries. While typically in developed countries, a user's first exposure to the internet would be on a personal computer and then later to a laptop and then a mobile phone, most Indian users have skipped the computer phase and jumped directly to owning a mobile phone. Because of growing access to cheap mobile phones, India remains one of the only countries where smartphone purchases are steadily growing, as compared to developed countries where the number of smartphone users has more or less plateaued.

Digital Payments and Instant Gratification

Access to any information you want right at your fingertips is a powerful influence. It means that users have more or less come to expect instantaneous fulfillment of any need that they might have. 'Patience' is no longer a virtue to be admired or aspired to. This instant gratification mindset has been further reinforced by 'same-day deliveries' and 'next-day deliveries' offered by e-commerce stores. The rise of digital payment avenues has made it even easier for users to take concrete action to any impulse purchase they might be on the verge of making. Most payment options today save your details, requiring you to only type in your security code to complete the payment. Payment apps powered by UPI have also halved the time required to make an online payment. Studies have repeatedly shown that shopping can give you a sudden boost of dopamine, the 'happiness' hormone. When it has become increasingly easy to get that serotonin surge, you can see why e-commerce usage and sales have been skyrocketing.

Preference for Convenience

Today's customer values their time and convenience above all else. For example, when a user visits your website, they don't want to work hard to get to the section they're interested in. They want to intuitively know how to navigate through it with minimum effort. Similarly, when a user wants to buy your product, they don't want to go through multiple steps before reaching the payment gateway. Another area where convenience has overshadowed all else is in the realm of brand loyalty. Even if a consumer has been repeatedly purchasing from your brand, if another brand claims to offer faster shipping times and a smoother return policy, that consumer will very likely not think twice about switching their allegiance.

The modern breed of consumers are living in a world that is rapidly changing every day. Even as recently as ten years ago, a lot of the technologies that have become part of us today were not heard of. Marketing strategies need to change just as rapidly to continue to attract consumers and retain them.

CHAPTER 6

Mirroring Bird Calls: Personalization of the Consumer Journey

The savannah is a birdwatcher's dream come true. With over 1000 species flying in the skies and perched on the trees, you can spot birds of virtually every colour here – if you know how to look. Some of the most elusive birds can often be coaxed into view through a series of well-timed bird calls. Guides will often use a mix of different bird sounds to attract different species of birds, cleverly manipulating the intensity and frequency of the calls depending upon the species.

This isn't all too different from what we do to attract our audience. The essence of advertising, whether online or offline, is understanding what your consumers want and fine tuning your messaging to appeal to them. In the era of mass messaging, how do you ensure that your communication is personalized?

David Ogilvy once said **"When people read your copy, they are alone. Pretend you are writing to each of them a letter on behalf of your client."** Coming to think of it, every customer is on a journey that starts from the moment they first learned about your brand to their first purchase, with each step leading to a path. As marketers, our job is to add value at each step for him, making the journey worthwhile as well as ensuring a smooth transition from awareness to conversion for the brand.

Prioritising & Personalisation – the Game Changer

The process of customer profiling and personalisation starts with setting a context of customer experience by distinguishing and prioritising customer segments, anchoring them to experiences that are exclusively crafted for them and guiding them through relevant customer journeys.

Personalisation is the key factor through which we can lead every individual customer journey to better customer experiences. Every piece of communication that you send out there needs to be relevant to the specific needs of your customer segments. In a nutshell, that's how you can optimise your marketing-spend efficiency.

Let's start with personalisation. Before you begin personalising experiences for each of your customer segments, you should delve upon the fact that all customers are not the same. They can be segregated into groups and the first step is to determine which group/s are more important to your business than others. The more accurately you select, segment, and prioritise your target customer groups, the easier the road ahead to conversion would be.

To understand prioritisation, let's dig into one effective method you can employ to prioritise your consumer segments; it is to examine their past experiences. Simple actions like analysing their interests in certain product categories, frequency of their visits to specific brand pages, etc. can help you determine their intent and stages they are in their purchase journey. There are tools (some are free) that enable you to collect and aggregate such relevant data points about your customers and their preferences such as buying history, geolocation, website-visit behavior, engagement with competitor brands, etc. Using these data, you can segregate your customers and prospects into different categories, prioritise them, and then personalise your communication, accordingly.

Customer Profiling, Buyer's Persona, and the All-Important Disparity!

Customer profiling is the process of preparing a detailed description of your target audience. It's similar to a buyer persona, however with a difference. Unlike the buyer's persona, it's not a fictional representation of your customers. Customer profiling is based on factual information like demographics, buying behaviors, geographic information, and more. A professionally designed customer profile benefits everyone who's involved in the marketing ecosystem in an organization. It's equally useful for product managers who are in charge of developing a new product or the strategists who would craft positioning strategies for the product/service.

Steps to create a customer profile:

- Define the problems that your business is trying to solve
- Design and analysis your customer journey map
- Explore data points related to your customer segments
- Collect and evaluate as much customer feedback as possible
- Build buyer personas
- Develop and finetune your offerings as per your buyers' personas

Buyer Personas

Buyer personas are developed using real answers from real customers and are always backed by detailed research. By creating a buyer's persona, brand custodians can navigate the landscape of their model customers.

The fictional characters are not just descriptions of your buyers, but they are characters developed on the basis of a collection of important insights about your customer profiles.

Here's a quick example of what happens when you look beyond demographics and design a buyer's persona for your brand.

Let's see if we can decide our marketing strategy to the following person with these demographics:

- Male
- Around 50 years old
- Born and lives in India
- Occupation – Politics
- Education – Master's Degree

This demographic profile actually identifies two people, Arvind Kejriwal and Rahul Gandhi, but as you know, They are different as chalk and cheese! You would think very differently while deciding your strategies to market your product to them.

In a nutshell, this is why you can't ignore a buyer's persona while designing your marketing strategy.

The Magic of Personalised Content

To make your content tailor-made for your customer segments, you can decide your explicit identifiers. For example, a newbie is identified from data points like – first visit, interaction with PPC landing page, the search engine uses, etc. Similarly, if you have data of a customer who has booked, say a luxury jungle safari, and you have an upselling proposition for a VIP membership for a hotel near his touring destination, you can tailor-make your content for him and can expect a much higher possibility of conversion than usual. It doesn't end there. If this customer is a safari enthusiast and his datapoint shows that he has booked multiple safaris, previously, sending them content about interesting upcoming safari events would instantly make him interested and engaged with your content.

Mapping your customers' journeys and analysing them carefully can help you to deliver the right experience to them and keep them delighted. A customer journey is the series of experiences that your customers go through during their purchase cycle which also includes all of their relations with your brand.

It will be prudent to remember that each customer journey map is different. Depending on the customer, their experience, and your business, the design will differ.

In recent years, there has been a paradigm shift in the manner content is used by brands for marketing purposes. In fact, we can say that we are in the middle of a content Tsunami and we are experiencing unparalleled growth in content production across all digital platforms. However, amid so much white noise, it becomes a challenge for us to produce the right kind of content that's personalized for our customer segments.

The question is how?

Here's how you can use audience profiling for a personalized content marketing strategy.

Auditing – To tap and engage with your customers who are at different stages of their buying journeys through answering their questions, evoking interest in them, and helping them to take decisions.

Profiling – As described earlier in this chapter, here you employ your data and prepare your data-driven customer profiling.

Create & publish personalised content – Here you leverage your customer profiling data and create or tweak your communication to meet the users' want and need.

One thing to remember, content personalisation is not a one-time job. Your content strategy has to keep evolving with the changing customer mindset and the changing aspects of the content publishing platforms. Stagnation is not an option!

So Where are We Heading with This?

It will not be wrong to say that the pinnacle of personalization is not here, yet! But we can see it coming our way for sure. With technology advancing every moment, it sure is an exciting time for the marketers to be experimental and innovative in the means of delivering personalised experience to each customer. With the power of data analytics, marketers are already equipped to create personalised experiences across moments, platforms, and stages.

Hyper-Personalization

Hyper personalisation is the next step to personalised marketing. The theory of it is based on the uses of artificial intelligence (AI) and real-time data. The approach of hyper-personalisation would enable the marketers to produce much relevant content to every user than it is possible through personalisation.

Personalisation is done through the incorporation of personal and transactional data points such as name, age, title, education, occupation, purchase history, etc., whereas hyper-personalisation goes one step further and by making use of real-time data and behavioral insights to create highly contextual content.

So why do we need hyper-personalisation?

The attention span of your customers is dwindling and fast! Give or take, you have about 5–6 seconds to capture their attention. So, unless you are delivering highly relatable content, you are scrolled up in no time.

Information overload makes consumers bounce back. Hence, they will be more likely to purchase from you if your offerings are personalised as per individual preferences.

App Personalisation

Taking it closer to the customers, marketers are exploring app personalisation too. There are some apps that give their customers options to take photos, tag, and save the product they love, and then they recommend their customers products as per their preferences.

Finally, we must understand that personalisation is passing fad or just another digital marketing trend, but it's the future of business. Gone are the days when personalisation started and ended with using an individual's name in an email. Time has come to provide user experiences at every platform and every stage that correlates to their unique interests through relevant content. As it is rightly said that the numbers don't lie, the future of business lies in understanding your customers through data-driven techniques and then creating unique experiences tailored to each one of your customers. This is and will remain the most effective way to build lasting customer relationships and drive loyalty.

Middle Funnel: Earning Your Audiences' Trust and Imparting more Knowledge on what Your Brand has to Offer

Now that your audience are aware of your brand, what are the strategies that can be used to position yourself as a go-to brand by earning the potential customer's trust? How can you navigate the consideration stage without selling them right off the bat?

In many instances, brands tend to view their assets as split into two groups: online and offline. However, consider the online world and the numerous forms of communication it offers. A blog on your website has a very different purpose from the display ads you're running. Because of this, your digital presence can actually be split into three types:

- Owned media
- Earned media
- Paid media

Owned media is any digital asset that you assert full control over. Think of it as the digital version of a brick-and-mortar store. Within your store, you are free to decorate your interiors the way you want, stock the products you like and take full control over what information your store assistants provide interested shoppers. In the digital world, the most common form of owned media is your company's website and to an extent, your social media profiles.

Earned media is coverage that your brand earns through building authority, credibility and goodwill in the space. For instance, if you create an incredible product that gets people talking about it on social media and spreading information through word-of-mouth, you've *earned* that. This is why earned media is one of the most coveted forms of digital marketing. It's not something you can exert control over, but once the ball gets rolling, there are few other strategies that provide greater results.

Paid media, on the other hand, *is* something that you can control – for a price. Paid media covers your digital advertising techniques that require budgets in order to perform. This form of advertising is highly effective in situations where you need to build awareness quickly and have to get the initial ball rolling.

In this section, we're going to cover owned media and paid media – and how to gain the greatest traction from these.

Part I:
Owned Media

Chapter 7

Summoning the Pack: Improving Findability with SEO and Content

The spotted hyena is quite possibly one of the most noisy animals in the Serengeti. Hyenas have an impressive range of vocals and each sound serves a specific purpose. One of the most important sounds hyenas make is the low 'whoop'. Often while hunting in packs, hyenas can become isolated and therefore, vulnerable. To mark its presence, the hyena will emit a long whoop to the other members of the pack. This whoop can help attract the pack and even identify which hyena it came from.

Content marketing fuelled by a strong SEO strategy is the 'whoop' that draws your audience to you. It helps your brand organically attract your audience, build trust and distinguish you from the competition. The right content, in a nutshell, can help you gather and strengthen your pack.

Imagine a marketing strategy that takes months to pay off, doesn't let you control who views your messaging, requires consistent hard work over a prolonged period of time and is still the most valuable strategy that exists. That encapsulates content marketing.

When you're trying to build a loyal base of customers, trust is the most important factor to build with them. A customer who does not completely trust that a health food brand is an expert on nutrition will not believe that they are using the choicest of organic ingredients in their products. When this trust deficit grows, you have a customer who will not be an advocate for your brand, who will not think of you as soon as they have a need and who will easily switch to a competitor when the opportunity arises.

One of the driving goals for any brand should be to maximise their customer's trust in them. But, like in every relationship, trust takes time and cannot be forced. On a first date, you can be as vocal as you'd like about all your winning qualities, but unless you consistently display these qualities through your actions, your date is unlikely to believe you.

The same principle holds when it comes to the relationship between a brand and its customers. Your ads can keep harping on about how you're the best in the business, but unless the customer sees for themselves that you are an expert in your space and that their needs are your topmost priority, they're unlikely to give you a second date.

Content, Actually, is All Around Us

At any given moment of the consumer decision making journey, the consumer in question has a dozen questions. Going back to the example of a health food brand, imagine you run an organic foods brand called Organixx. Your consumer would have a lot of doubts before they even come to know about your brand. Supposing you have a health drink that consists of exotic berries sourced from the forests of South America, herbs grown in the remotest parts of India and the highest quality of protein and fat you can possibly find. Chances are, your customer isn't going to search for this product right off the bat. Instead, the typical progression of questions your customer has might look something like this:

- How unhealthy are sodas for you?
- What are good substitutes for soda?

- What ingredients should a healthy drink have?
- What are the benefits of South American berries?
- Are herbs good for your health?
- How can you get healthy protein and fat into your diet?
- What are the best health drinks in India?
- Is Organixx a good brand?

It's only after this long journey does the consumer actually uncover a need and start weighing their options. The outcome of this journey depends largely upon how present you have been through it all. If you had a blog that catered to each of these questions and showed up every time your consumer had a question, they automatically start believing in your information long before they're even considering purchasing from your brand. At the end, when they are looking to make a purchase, which would be the most likely decision they would make? Your brand who has consistently supported them throughout this journey or a competitor brand they don't have the same level of trust with? Clearly, content marketing might be a long-term, effort-intensive strategy, but the dividends are well worth the effort.

But that begs the question, what exactly comprises content marketing? To put it simply, content marketing is essentially any form of communication from your brand to your customer. It differs from ads because unlike ads, the goal of content marketing is not to *sell*, but to *inform*. You aren't creating content specifically to tout the advantages of your brand, but you are trying to provide useful and relevant information to a customer that satisfies your query.

Thus, while your ad copies might look something like this: *Shop from Organixx.com for lightning deals and free shipping!* Your blog copy might look something like this: *10 benefits of following an organic diet.*

Content marketing can and does take on many forms. Largely, there are four major formats of content marketing:

- Textual: Any form of written content comes under this category. Informative blogs, in-depth pillar content, email marketing to nurture leads, your website content and even educational social media content comes under this category. Textual content is often considered the most widely prevalent forms of content marketing.

- Visual: While textual content can be one of the best resources of information, some users prefer to consume content through a visual medium. Infographics and videos are excellent forms of visual content marketing. They can easily capture the attention of a user and offer ample space for creativity.

- Interactive: One of the best ways to gain the interest of a consumer is to get them to engage with you. Interactive content like quizzes, tools and polls are informative and also require active participation by your users. This can help them build higher recall of your brand.

- Audio: A quickly-emerging form of content marketing is podcasts. Podcasts are a wonderful, cost-effective way to reach your consumers on new platforms. The key here is to create a podcast on something that is extremely relevant for your customers so that they'll actually want to tune in each time to catch your latest show.

Leading the Horse to the Water

In the online space, the philosophy of "build and they will come" goes right out of the window. Even if you build a powerful content strategy, there is one major catch – your consumers might never come across it. After all, your website is one of thousands of others that cover similar topics. For every idea that you have, dozens of other websites have already written about it. In this saturated, competitive space, how do you lead your consumers to your website? In order to do this, we need to take a step back and understand how consumers even find new websites or sources of information.

In the Wizard of Oz, Dorothy and her motley crew of travel companions trekked across dangerous forests and fought evil witches in their quest to reach Oz, the Great and Powerful, the keeper of all knowledge in the world. In our world, Oz is right at our fingertips. Search engines have become the single greatest driver behind the Age of Information we currently live in. If you want people visiting your website, consuming your content and learning more about your brand, search engines in general – and Google in particular – are the ultimate way to lead them there.

However, search engines are also notoriously difficult to rank on. Hundreds of thousands of websites compete with each other for just 10 spots – the first page of Google. And as we've seen, hundreds of websites are publishing content around topics similar to yours. So why should Google rank your website ahead of all of these? The basic philosophy is simple: understand what Google is looking for and make sure your website ticks those boxes.

In reality, of course, it's a lot more complex than that.

The art of helping your content rank on Google – Search Engine Optimization – can largely be broken down into two main aspects:

On-Page SEO

What is it: Optimizing elements on the actual pages of your website so that they rank higher on Google.

What it covers: Including the right keywords in your content, ensuring the right heading tags are assigned, continuously monitoring the page for any technical errors that can affect Google's ranking of your page and fixing them immediately. The easier it is for Google to comb through your website, the more likely it is that you will rank.

Off-Page SEO

What is it: Activities done on external websites to improve the rankings of your website.

What it covers: Building backlinks (links from other websites to your website) forms a bulk of off-page SEO. Google sees every backlink as a token of trust in your content, therefore, the higher the number of backlinks you have, the higher the chances of you ranking. The other big part of off-page SEO is content amplification, which refers to posting links to your website on other platforms like social media to increase its visibility and traffic.

> **Case Study: How we implemented SEO strategies for overall organic growth for MFine**
>
> **Industry:** Healthcare
>
> **Objective:** To increase overall organic growth with focus on increasing relevant traffic (users looking for online doctor consultations).
>
> **Strategy**: We suggested aggressive SEO techniques that improved the visibility of their website. The top strategies include:
>
> - On-page and off-page SEO techniques
> - Building high-quality external backlinks
> - Extensive CTR analysis to improve the rankings on a weekly basis
> - Hyper optimisation of key pages with long-form content that included highly competitive keywords.
> - Improving the UX of the site for a seamless experience
> - Improving the speed of the site
>
> In addition to this we created 30 informative and content-heavy pages on the top medical conditions to increase online doctor consultations on the website and app across the 23 specialities and super-specialities offered by MFine. We used the following strategies to increase brand awareness through the guides

- In-depth keyword research to choose medical conditions based on high search volume and low difficulty.
- Each medical guide offers seamless UX with CTAs to consult with doctors at relevant places.
- Content vetted by doctors with valuable information on symptoms, treatment, precautions and surgical procedures – adhering to Google's EAT guidelines.

We also built a holistic microsite with authoritative and reliable content to get parents to consult a pediatrician for their child through mfine.. We identified close to 800 child health and nutrition-related problems, which fueled our content marketing strategy for the entire microsite.

The microsite included two interactive tools: 'Child BMI Calculator' and 'Child Growth Calculator'. These tools were a powerful lead generation technique as parents had to submit their contact details in order to get the results.

Business Impact:

Through this multifaceted content marketing strategy we got:

- 1) 149.34% increase in organic clicks in Oct – Dec 20' vs Oct – Dec 19'
- 2) Ranking in page 1 for 1000 target keywords in 3–4 months
- 3) 37% increase in backlinks and 125% increase in referring domains
- 4) Organic traffic was driven by medical guides, health packages, medicine pages, parenting pillars and the COVID-based pages.

New Avenues for Discoverability

For a very long time, Google has remained the Big Daddy of search engines – to a point where 'search engine' became synonymous with 'Google'. As a result, most SEO strategies focused on optimizing for Google alone. Today, however, the way consumers search is very different. They have specialized platforms where they search for specific requirements. Modern-day SEO strategies need to be able to optimize for these new platforms in order to be successful.

Largely, the major avenues where users perform searches include:

YouTube: YouTube has been called the world's second largest search engine. This has largely been driven by the wealth of information that is now available on YouTube. What used to be a platform for entertainment has now become an ecosystem in itself. Whether you're looking for information, entertainment or inspiration, you're sure to find a YouTube video that matches your needs. With the popularity of the platform, the competition has also increased massively. Ranking on YouTube requires a careful YouTube strategy – one that incorporates improving the quality of content, including the right keywords in the tags, titles and descriptions and writing catchy video titles among other things.

App Stores: The app market has become incredibly diverse and sophisticated. Most brands today also have an app and there's an app for practically any need that you might have. The competition to rank on the App Store and Play Store have also become fierce. Higher organic app installs can lead to greater ROI for your brand. Ranking for apps is improved through a process called App Store Optimization (ASO). This includes optimization of various elements like your app title, short description and long description with the right keywords. It also includes improving the appearance of the app listing by adding informative screenshots, videos and user reviews.

E-commerce: In 2009, when Bing was first launched, there was much talk about it de-throning Google and becoming the next big search engine. Today, however, the real threat to Google might not be coming from another traditional search engine, but an e-commerce giant: Amazon. Users today often skip Google entirely when they're looking for specific products and go directly to an e-commerce website. E-commerce SEO involves using the right keywords in your product description, adding the right images and improving reviews of the product,

Pinterest: If you've made a new recipe, tried out a new DIY project or given your room a new makeover recently, you might have gone directly to Pinterest to find inspiration. Pinterest has virtually replaced Google Image Search and is becoming one of the best avenues for discoverability. This is especially true for websites that fall in the categories of Health, Food, Travel and Fashion. Pinterest SEO involves categorizing your pins into relevant boards, adding optimized descriptions and the right hashtags.

Effort vs Result

One of the main hurdles preventing brands from investing in a full-fledged SEO and content strategy is the time and effort that goes into building one. To be clear, SEO and content don't offer quick wins. They require a sustained effort over a significant time period in order to see results. For a brand, the dilemma is obvious: why invest in a long-term strategy when you can invest in paid advertising that reaches exactly the right audience practically overnight?

To answer this question, it all boils down to a single word: sustainability. Yes, an organic strategy takes time, but once the gears are in motion, they are unstoppable. When your website starts seeing organic traffic overtaking paid traffic, you can bring your ad budgets to a complete standstill and still see massive traction.

In order to understand the impact of a strong SEO strategy, you don't have to look too far back in history. With the onset of the COVID-19 pandemic and the ensuing lockdown, almost every company saw an abrupt halt to their paid activities. In this scenario, you had two types of outcomes:

1> Companies who had a weak organic strategy with a negligible portion of their total website audience coming from organic sources saw their website performance almost flatline. These companies would have to start from scratch once the lockdown lifted in order to gain traction again.

2> Companies who had a strong organic strategy saw a slight dip as organic searches went down, but since most of their content was evergreen, they still had a good number of organic visits to their website. These companies continued to build awareness among their audience despite the lockdown and would emerge with greater brand equity once restrictions were lifted.

> **Case Study: How We Built a Lockdown-Proof Organic Strategy for ZestMoney**
>
> **Industry:** Banking and Financial services
>
> **Objective:**
>
> ZestMoney is a first of its kind payment platform which allows users to make large purchases without a credit card. Since users don't require a credit card, debit card or credit score to be eligible for ZestMoney, this platform has opened up the possibilities of affordable EMI payments to thousands of Indians.
>
> In India, there are only 47 million credit card users as of 2019, leaving Zest with an objective to reach out to a huge potential target audience.
>
> **Strategy:**
>
> To increase Zest's visibility and brand awareness, we came up with a three-pronged strategy:
>
> 1. **Findability**
>
>   In order to understand where ZestMoney stood vis-a-vis its competitors, we conducted comprehensive competitor keyword research to understand what queries were

driving traffic to competitor websites. This helped our organic strategy in two ways:

i. It helped us optimize existing pages with new and relevant keywords to increase their search rankings

ii. It helped us identify potential high-interest areas that we hadn't covered and develop new content that would drive traffic and leads to the website

2. User-centric content

A majority of Zest's audience were 'no-credit' or 'new-to-credit' consumers. These consumers, most of whom hailed from non-metro cities, had strong materialistic aspirations due to their exposure to different lifestyles on social media. But without a strong credit score or a valid credit card, they did not have the means to actually make these purchases. We leveraged this insight to develop a user-centric blog called 'Shop Smartly'. The 'Shop Smartly' blog offers users informative listicles of the best gadgets, fashion items and holiday packages in different price ranges along with details on how they could purchase them using ZestMoney. This blog soon became one of the biggest drivers of non-brand traffic to the website.

3. In-depth guides

Starting an EMI is a long-term commitment and one that a user can make only after they have gathered enough information about the plan and have trust in the EMI provider. To cater to their needs, we developed two comprehensive pillar pages. Both these pages merged informative content along with step-by-step instructions on how users could avail of Zest's no-cost EMI plans. The full-funnel approach on these pages helped drive significant organic traffic for high-intent keywords.

Business impact:

- Total non-brand keywords in **positions 1–3** increased by **45%**
- Total number of non-brand keywords **ranking on page 1** increased by **30%**
- **32%** increase in total backlinks and a **60%** increase in referring domains
- Organic traffic driven by the blogs and guides remained stable during the lockdown period and bounced back to pre-lockdown numbers within a few weeks of the economy opening back up

No matter which sector you fall into, a powerful organic marketing strategy can deliver higher ROI, encourage greater brand loyalty and serve as the ultimate insurance plan against the ups and downs of the market.

CHAPTER 8

Navigating the Skies: Building Seamless User Experience

Visit the Serengeti between the months of November and April, and you'd be wise to turn your eyes up to the skies. Birdwatching in the savannahs is always a colourful, chirpy affair, but during these months, avid bird watchers can spot migratory birds flying in from North Africa and distant Europe. Despite having to traverse thousands of kilometres, migratory birds never get lost. Scientists believe that this is because the bird's body is built for navigation. Its eyes and brain can detect 'north' and its beak helps it stay true to its path.

Think of your website as a new land that visitors must find a way to navigate through. The easier you make it for them to find their way through, the longer they will spend on it. Like the migratory bird, your website needs to be built for easy navigation. This is only possible through an intuitive understanding of user experience.

Ever since the dawn of time, human beings have been trying to make sense of the world around us. One of the most defining characteristics of the human race is that we don't just adapt to our surroundings, we try to *change* them so that they meet our needs. Thousands of years ago, hunter-gatherer tribes would burn large tracts of forest land to make it easier to create a settlement and find food. In essence, they were modifying their environment so that they could understand it better and gain more use from it. Fast forward a few millennia later and their descendents were building homes laid out in a way that would enable each member of the household to have their own private space and yet have ample room to socialize with each other when they wanted to. Moving even further into the future, we enter the Age of Technology, where human beings are trying to find the best way to arrange virtual elements in a manner that makes the most sense for those who have to navigate through it. Throughout the history of mankind, the means have kept evolving but the end-goal has remained the same: to improve a user's experience with an object or place.

Far too often, user experience is viewed through the lens of modern-day terminology: wireframes, responsiveness, adaptability, and more. However, at the crux of user experience is a very basic, almost primitive, need that each one of us has: to understand our surroundings. When we lose sight of this goal, we create user interfaces that are overly stylized and offer no real value to the end-user.

The Evolution of User Interface

Over the years, as humans have become more familiar with different technology and our interactions in themselves have changed, user interface has also evolved. Some of the earliest references to user interface and user experience can be found in the ancient Chinese philosophy of Feng Shui and Indian philosophy of Vastu. Both these schools of thought broke down every object in the world into five main elements: fire, water, wind, earth and space. According to their principles, each of these elements had to be arranged in a way that would improve the flow of energy.

Modern user interface and its evolution can be understood in much the same way. A standard website has a few key elements: a menu of all the pages, the main banner communication, a specific call-to-action, a form to capture information and a way to move between the different pages of the website. The manner in which these elements are arranged can either enable a user to engage with the website or hinder them from it. The fundamental goal of User Experience is to find the best way to arrange these elements in a manner that makes the most sense for the user. The exact way to do this keeps evolving because users themselves keep evolving.

From Skeuomorphism to Flat Design

Think back to the earliest days when you first used a computer or a smartphone. Many of the elements on your screen were essentially replicas of real-life objects in your world. The music player on early smartphones resembled a 3-D stereo system. The email symbol was a 3-D lifelike image of a real envelope. The calculator on your phone looked almost exactly like the actual calculator you were used to. The 3-D nature of these designs belonged to a school of UX design called Skeuomorphism. The goal of Skeuomorphism was to replicate the real world as much as possible. The need for this was obvious. People weren't used to interacting with hitherto real-life figures on a flat screen. In order to help them acclimatize to their new flat screen, their new virtual world had to resemble the one they were used to.

But as users started to get more digitally mature, the need for skeuomorphism began to take a backseat. Unlike at the start of the Skeuomorphic Era, users were now more comfortable with their flat screens than with their everyday real-life objects. Suddenly, pinching to zoom, tapping to select and swiping to change became as natural as old hand gestures like waving and clapping. Users no longer had to be educated on how to navigate through the virtual world, they were now masters of it. With the need for familiarity no longer a motivation behind UX design, UX specialists were free to incorporate a more minimalist approach when designing interfaces. This led to the era of Flat Design.

The rise of minimalism in UX design corresponded with the popularity of minimalism in our everyday lives. People no longer had patience for clutter; they knew exactly what they wanted and anything that had no functional purpose was merely superfluous. Because of this, website designs started getting cleaner, navigational elements were kept simple and unintrusive. Thus, volume buttons changed from round dials to sliders. The Kindle e-reader started to display just plain text on the page rather than the overly-stylized attempts to recreate an actual book evident in some of the earliest e-readers. Flat designs were marked by their use of squares and grids in page layouts. There was another reason for this: more users than ever before were accessing the internet primarily through their phone. Because of this, website designs had to seamlessly switch from larger desktop screens to smaller phone screens. Most skeuomorphic designs required a lot of space, something that phone screens simply could not provide.

Designing for the Digital World

There's no one-size-fits-all formula when it comes to UX for the modern internet user. This is also because there is no single type of internet user. With the expansion of the internet, we're seeing users from different countries, cultural backgrounds, education and more coming online. Intuitive UX design, therefore, will have to conform to what they require. For example, Google's Designing for Accessibility study uncovered that vernacular users require larger descriptive icons. A typical urban internet user, on the other hand, might find that too distracting. Thus, effective UX requires a complete understanding of the user in order to design an experience that appeals to them.

In the simplest form, UX design can be broken down into the following stages:

Stage 1: Establishing User Personas

Understanding who is going to be visiting the website, interacting with the app or using the device is the first step of UX design. Only once you have a thorough understanding of your user personas can you design an experience for them that is intuitive and engaging. Our expectations from UX are largely shaped by our culture, technological maturity and pain points. It's just as imperative for UX designers to understand these personas as it is for branding and marketing teams.

Stage 2: Building the Information Hierarchy

For every website and app, there is a lot of different information you want to put forward to the user. When done right, a website's UX can capture a user's attention, encourage them to explore other pages on the website and nudge them towards taking action. The extent to which this is done depends upon the information hierarchy. An information hierarchy is a way that all information on the website and each individual page will be structured. Based on this, the sitemap of the website and the wireframes of the individual pages will be created.

Stage 3: Testing Usability

A key component of UX is continuously monitoring its effectiveness. A large part of UX design is making hypotheses. You assume that a user will navigate the website in a certain way and build each page based on your assumption. Once these pages are live, you need to constantly go back and check if your hypothesis is proved true or false. Heatmaps, for instance, can show you exactly how users engage with your website. You might gain incredible insights into what's working and what's not once you see actual interactions on your page.

Virtual Experiences, Real Consequences

User experience is often seen in terms of its aesthetic value alone. Sure, a good website is a nice asset to have, but ultimately, your sales come down to the quality of your product or service, right? Well, not necessarily. Most users will not even try your product if the road to buying it isn't smooth and free of obstacles. Bad UX can often take two main forms: either a website has so many elements and graphics that a user is overwhelmed and unsure of what step to take next or a website can be too sparse and a user can be confused about how to navigate through it. When either of these things happen, your company's bottom line will be impacted in a big way. Your website or app will bring in fewer conversions, sales figures will drop and your brand perception can dip.

The history and future of user experience is far from linear. As technology in the field of Augmented Reality and Virtual Reality become more sophisticated, the need for skeuomorphic design has emerged stronger than ever. But whatever the shape of form that UX takes, the crux of it remains understanding your user and providing them with the most seamless experience that guides them towards taking a desired action.

CHAPTER 9

Conducting the Orchestra: Storytelling Through Videos

If you camp out in the Serengeti, you won't need your alarm to wake you up. Every morning as the daylight starts to break, the birds start to sing at the top of their lungs, a phenomenon known as the dawn chorus. If you listen attentively, the dawn chorus is actually nature's biggest musical extravaganza. Bird species perched on the highest branches, who are the first to be hit by the sun's rays, sing first, followed by the lower branches in hierarchy. The dawn chorus is also unique to different parts of the world. The most sensitive bird lovers understand that the dawn chorus is a layered story waiting to be unfolded.

No matter what platform a user is on, they ultimately want to be entertained, they want to be told a story. And what better way to spin a story that is as textured and unique as the dawn chorus, than a good video? It's little wonder then that video is one of the breakout content formats of the decade.

Human beings love watching videos – that's an indisputable truth. This fact is hardly new either; right from the 1980s when The Buggles sang their one and only hit to forty years later when we gravitate towards video-driven social platforms, one thing has remained constant: our love for video content trumps all else. What has changed of late is the way in which videos are being used and consumed. Initially, video content was one of the most investment-heavy forms of content. You needed the right studio, the right equipment and the right post-production team to create a good video. All of these factors drove up the cost of making a video, making it a strategy only established brands could afford to leverage.

Today, however, many of those barriers have come crashing down. Audiences are now more interested in the quality of the content rather than the quality of the production. In fact, overly-produced videos can sometimes backfire as viewers might perceive the brand as being disingenuous. Another factor enabling the growth of video content is the decrease in the cost of production itself. Most smartphones today are able to record HD videos that rival high-end cameras. Thus, any brand can create video content and every brand should.

The Changing Why's of Video Marketing

Another effect of the decreasing cost of video production is the very goal of video marketing. Initially, videos were often viewed as extensions of TV commercials. They were a one-way form of communication used to announce new launches, new product features or new campaigns. Essentially, videos were a means for brands to talk about themselves. Today, video marketing looks completely different. Brands aren't just creating videos to promote themselves, they're also creating them to inform and engage with their audience.

Because of this, video marketing has taken on many roles and can achieve a number of different business objectives. A video isn't just a means to increase awareness among consumers about your brand, but it's also a way to share relevant information with them in a visually rich and engaging format. Through videos, brands can reach users at practically every stage of the funnel. Videos around generic topics of interest to target audiences can reach top-of-the-funnel users, videos around the product USPs are ideal for the middle funnel and video testimonials and case studies can convert users at the bottom of the funnel. Videos can also improve customer experience and retention, especially demo videos and walkthroughs. Thus videos aren't just a standalone strategy for social media, they can also be used on landing pages, blogs and email campaigns for better results.

Ingredients of a Powerful Video Strategy

Video marketing for middle funnel users differs from video marketing for other stages of the funnel for a number of reasons. The purpose of videos at the top and bottom of the funnel is to inform. The purpose of videos in the middle of the funnel is to engage users and capture their attention, a much more challenging task.

It's difficult to pinpoint a failsafe formula that will help you create viral videos every time. Oftentimes, a video clicks with the audience for no discernible reason and becomes instantly popular. But while certain facets of successful video marketing might be left to fate, there are still several factors that are completely within our control.

Uncovering the Right Audience Insight

The most successful comedians aren't the ones with the smartest wordplay or the most unpredictable punchline; they're the ones who shed light on a relatable aspect of life each one of us have experienced. The same philosophy goes for video marketing too. In order to create a video that strikes a chord with viewers, you need to understand how users think, feel and behave around a specific product, brand or segment. You need to delve into their psyche and uncover past memories that are indelibly tied to the product. Gokul Santol, for example, has a powerful floral fragrance that is usually the first thing that comes to a person's mind when they think about the product. This fragrance immediately triggers nostalgic feelings of the past when their parents would get them ready for school with a quick pat of Gokul Santol's talcum powder on their face for good measure. This user insight became the driving theme behind the brand's new digital campaign.

Once you have the user insight, you can tie it back with your brand objectives to drive quantifiable results; however that insight remains the bedrock of the video campaign.

There is a, however, a balance you need to strike between relatability and originality. While you do want the concept of your video to be familiar to your audience, you want the overall treatment and storyline of the video to be completely original, in a way that grabs their attention. Striking this balance can make your video unforgettable.

Case Study: How We Used Personalized Video Content to Deliver Higher Engagement & Leads for TATA Mutual Funds

Industry: Banking and Finance

Objective: With a plethora of tax saving investment options available, our aim was to make Tata Mutual's tax saving funds stand out amongst the rest.

Strategy: Considering that a topic related to tax could be boring and at the same time daunting, we kept in mind what the viewers could relate to by engaging them with topics that were trending. The ultimate goal was to receive quality leads that would lead to successful conversions.

Keeping this in mind, we conceptualised a video campaign that would break through the clutter and stand out in the competitive mutual funds space in India. Comprising four short videos based around a common theme, the video campaign highlighted the importance of investing in an ELSS tax-saving scheme.

All these ads have protagonists across demographics such as a working woman, a management trainee, a sportsman and an executive relaxing in his home. used everyday scenarios that everyone, no matter what their age or gender, can identify with, for instance, shopping for groceries and ordering a pizza. This idea was distilled into the catchy hashtag #NoToKatauti.

Our social media strategy too echoed the same tone and voice. We leveraged trending topics like the most recent movies release, election results and tied it back to tax savings

The campaign was extended to offline as well and was it being advertised in major daily newspapers across the country.

Business Impact:

By hitting the right chords, we were able to achieve outstanding results on this campaign.

- 94 million impressions for our videos
- 5 million interactions cumulatively
- 7,500+ leads generated
- 3.9 million total video views achieved

Choosing the Right Video Format

The platform on which we view a video can make a huge difference in the way we perceive it. There's a reason why we still pay money to watch movies on the big screen despite knowing we can watch it for free on our laptops or TVs a few weeks later. Choosing the right video format and platform to showcase your video is also important because user's visit different platforms to meet different requirements. They might watch videos on Instagram to be entertained, videos on YouTube to be informed and videos on LinkedIn to improve their skills. If your video doesn't match their intentions, then it won't work regardless of how good the idea behind it is.

One thing that is for certain is that no matter what purpose your video serves, it needs to be optimized for mobile screens. An increasing number of users are viewing videos primarily through their phones and if your video isn't tailor-made for the tiny screen, it might not gain much traction.

Effortless Translation from Script to Shoot to Edit

The first step in creating a powerful video is successfully spinning a convincing script from a single insight. The script needs to be written in a language that is familiar to your audience, using lingo that they themselves use. A script for a video also needs to take into account two major factors: one, your audience needs to be engaged from beginning to end and two, your audience is easily distracted and has a limited attention span. Both of these factors also need to be taken into account at the editing table. You have to approach the script and the raw video with a ruthless pair of trimming scissors. Any extra clutter that distracts from the main storyline of the video needs to be cut, leaving only a concise video that is captivating from beginning to end.

Conjuring Up a Compelling Title

The first impression users have of your video isn't necessarily the opening shots, but its title. This is a unique feature of videos on social media because in no other video format can users choose whether they want to watch a video or not depending upon what it's titled. In fact, in most cases, they wouldn't even be aware of what the video is titled. On social media, however, an unusual or interesting video title can make a user stop scrolling through the newsfeed and continue to watch the video to see what it's about.

Video marketing presents a powerful way for brands to spin powerful stories, spread information and build a strong connection with audiences in every stage of the funnel. The extent to which marketers are able to tap into this potential depends upon how accurate their customer profile and user insights are.

CHAPTER 10

Building a Formidable Network: Crafting a Social Media Strategy

Individual meerkats are tiny creatures, merely a blip when compared to larger animals in the Serengeti such as hippos and wild buffaloes. But the true strength of meerkats lies in the extensive networks they create – it's the key to their survival. For instance, when some members of the colony are out foraging for food, other members act as 'sentries', looking out for any potential threats. These strong networks have allowed the tiny meerkats to outlive most of their larger cohabitants in the savannah.

The biggest and strongest network of our age is social media. Here, individuals can come together as a formidable force and develop strong bonds. A strong social media strategy will build you a tribe that will become the lifeblood of your brand and help it outlast competitors.

You don't need shocking statistics or impressive case studies to understand the central role social media plays in each of our lives today. All you need to do is retrace your day and think about just how many times you opened your phone or laptop and scrolled through our feed, either on Instagram, Facebook or LinkedIn. If the birth of the internet spawned a whole new world of information and accessibility, the advent of social media fostered the cultural zeitgeist in this new Age of the Internet. Through social media, virtually anyone can express their opinions to a massive audience. The former gatekeepers of information, such as news editors, have become redundant in the completely democratic world of social media. While this has also sparked an important worldwide debate about regulation of content on social media, there is no doubt that these platforms are among the most powerful sources of information and influence in today's world.

For a brand, it isn't a question of whether you should be on social media, but how best to do so. After all, the key to a successful marketing strategy is to carve a niche in the mindspace of your customers and what better way to do so than engaging with them on platforms where they spend a huge chunk of their time?

But while most brands do understand the importance of being on social media, not all approach it in the right way. Far too often, a brand's social media strategy is a haphazard collection of posts with no clear direction to it. While social media does offer a way for your brand to get more personal and less formal, there still needs to be a clear strategy that underlies your social presence.

The same advantage of social media that offers limitless potential for brands to dabble in as many trends as they want to and post as frequently as they want to can also lead to a risk of the overall social media strategy appearing disjointed.

The secret to developing a winning social media strategy that gains hearts and followers lies in following five fail-safe steps.

Step #1 Set Your Goals in Advance

In social media marketing, as with any business strategy, subsequent actions flow from a single overarching goal. Setting in place a concrete goal ensures that your approach to social media is linear and focused on achieving something specific. Depending upon the stage your business is in, your goals from social media might look something like this:

i. **To gain more followers:** If your business is new or if you've just started your social media page, then your immediate objective might be to gain more followers. At this point you aren't looking primarily for conversions, but you are looking at more people following you and viewing your posts.

   Some of the best ways to achieve this objective is to run referral programs. For example, you might offer a special discount to users who tag their friends in a comment or who get 5 of their friends to follow your account.

ii. **To build brand awareness:** If your product is new or if you are trying to grab attention away from a competitor, then creating awareness will be your primary objective. In this approach, the main purpose behind your social media strategy will be to gain mindshare and carve a niche in your field.

   Since most users won't be aware of your brand or product at this stage, creating posts around your brand's values and generic information about the product and its advantages will help you meet your goal.

iii. **To increase engagement:** Do you already have a sizable number of followers but that doesn't seem to be translating in the engagement on the posts you put up? This might be because your posts either don't resonate with your audience or they don't see any incentive in engaging with the posts. From a brand's perspective, audience engagement is crucial because it keeps users invested in your brand and more likely to convert down the line. Audience engagement can also translate into increased brand reach.

   If increasing audience engagement is your goal, then posts which have a clear question and launching user-generated content campaigns with clear incentives can help get the ball rolling.

iv. **To increase conversions/sales:** If you are looking at converting your social media clout into sales, then your strategy needs to adapt. A user who follows your brand might not necessarily ever convert into a paying customer.

Ensuring new product launches, sales and offers are constantly updated on your social media profiles is essential to push users into making a purchase. You should even consider adding special promo codes for your followers to nudge them into taking action.

Unlike your marketing objective, your social media goals are dynamic and will keep changing based on which stage your business is in or on the season. The key is to ensure that you define your goal for that period early on so you can create a targeted social media strategy to help achieve your objective.

Step #2 Gain Clear User Insights

If there has been one constant refrain throughout this book, it's that audience insights is one of the most powerful assets you can have. Social media is arguably one of the most important platforms to gain and leverage consumer insights. This is because on social media, you are ultimately looking to build a tribe, speaking to users in the lingo they use, sharing interests they have and offering them content they're looking for. Conversely, social media can also be used to *gain* these precious audience insights. There are a number of social media analytics platforms that can help you gain insights into your audience.

All of the content you put out and your tonality on different platforms needs to match what your users are looking for.

Step #3 Perform a Competitor Analysis

Whatever your end goal is from social media marketing, one of your main objectives will be to divert a user's attention away from your competition and encourage them to switch their allegiance to you instead. In order to do that, you need to first understand what your competitors are currently doing. There is, however, a thin line between inspiration and plagiarism. The latter can undermine the credibility of your brand and alienate your followers. Rather than copying what your competitors are doing point for point, you should instead look at their broad strategy, analyse what's working for them and come up with points on how you can top that.

In some cases, you might want to do the polar opposite of what your competitors are currently doing in order to differentiate your brand and break the clutter. That's an excellent strategy too. Either way, you need to first understand what competition you're up against before you devise a strategy to beat them.

Step #4 Choose the Right Metrics to Track

Social media offers a wealth of metrics, but you need to zero in on the ones that best align with your original goals. For example, gaining more likes and followers might be a good metric to track if your goal was to increase engagement and reach, however, if your goal was to drive conversions, then they might not be as useful.

In general, the following metrics are best suited to these respective goals:

Increase reach	Increase in followers/subscribers and views
Increase engagement	Higher likes and comments, hashtag performance
Increase conversions	Website visits, form fills
Improve customer experience and retention	Increase in reviews and decrease in response times

Step #5 Follow a Consistent Aesthetic

Your entire social media presence should look cohesive and instantly recognizable. This consistency can be in terms of the colour palette used, tonality of posts, themes followed or a combination of all of these factors. Once you identify these factors, all teams involved in content creation for your social media handles should follow them religiously. This is absolutely crucial in order to develop a strong brand identity online and develop a connection with your audience.

Social media is the biggest stage your brand can ever have. It's the metaphorical soap box from where you can broadcast your brand's message to a massive audience. By getting the critical foundational elements of your social media strategy in place, you stand to gain a huge, faithful following who can become some of the biggest advocates and ambassadors for your brand.

Part II:
Paid Media

CHAPTER 11

Spotting the Watering Holes: Choosing the Right Platforms to Target

The Serengeti is a pretty crowded stretch of grassland so chances are you will spot wildlife no matter where or when you go. But if you want to spot the most elusive animals, you need to choose your strategy carefully. You need to carefully understand the habits and routines of these animals if you want to be in the right place at the right time. Venturing out at the break of dawn and finding the most popular watering holes gives you the best chances of witnessing these animals in their natural habitat and at their most active.

The internet is also a similarly crowded space where your brand can easily be everywhere all the time. But just because you can, that doesn't make it the best approach. Choosing the right paid platforms for your brand to advertise on involves first taking a step back and understanding the psyche of consumers who use these platforms.

Digital marketing has a huge number of ad platforms and ad formats at your disposal, but sometimes, this might result in the problem of plenty. No good ever came out of shooting everywhere and hoping for the best and the same applies to your digital marketing strategy. Just because you *can* advertise on a huge range of platforms, doesn't mean you *should*. After all, your target audience isn't the entire digital universe, it's only a specific segment of them. Your job as a digital marketer is to identify where in the virtual world your audience is most active, what is their intent while using these platforms and how best can your ads match it.

With these key factors in mind, let's take a deeper look into some of the most popular advertising platforms available today.

Facebook

Facebook is one of the best all-rounder platforms to promote your product or brand. While other social media platforms usually cater to a specific audience segment or need, Facebook has a largely universal appeal. There have been some concerns that Facebook is losing its footing among the incoming Generation Z, and this is not untrue. If your target audience consists largely of users above the age of 40, then Facebook remains one of the best ways to reach them. However, on a larger scale, Facebook does have a very broad, diverse audience that you can target.

It's important to remember that Facebook is best used as a platform to drive brand awareness, create interest and educate users. Most users on the platform have a low purchase intent and might not necessarily purchase your product right at that point of time. However, the gamut of targeting options Facebook offers does ensure that your brand will gain awareness among the right audience and will trigger the start of their purchase journey.

Instagram

Instagram is a purely visual medium and thus works best for brands whose offerings can be easily represented visually. Brands in segments like retail, e-commerce, food, fitness, and wellness are best suited for Instagram. This platform is hugely popular among users below 40, particularly Gen Z and millennials.

When using Instagram ads for your business, it's important to remember the mindset with which users approach the platform. The visually stunning posts that pepper our feeds are testament to the fact that Instagram presents an aspirational lifestyle. The extent to which your brand can fit into this perception of the consumer as their ideal self will determine your success on Instagram. While Instagram is also a great avenue to build awareness, its users do have a higher purchase intent than on Facebook. If your brand falls in the realm of fashion, food, nutrition or similar segments, Instagram ads can be a great way to increase awareness as well as sales.

LinkedIn

LinkedIn was an oft neglected platform, but its time has finally come. To be clear, LinkedIn is not for every brand, but that's one of its strengths. The platform offers a niche audience that actively uses it to expand their professional knowledge, improve their careers and grow their network. As a result, when it comes to B2B brands, there are few platforms that can be more effective than LinkedIn.

Most B2B brands have a long sales cycle and a very targeted audience base. They aren't looking to reach as many people as they can; they only want to speak to the main decision makers of an organization. This fits in perfectly with LinkedIn's own demographics. A majority of LinkedIn users have a college degree and the ones that are most active on the platform tend to be those in senior management levels. India is also a growing market for LinkedIn, contributing to the second largest number of users after the US.

Brands should look at LinkedIn as a way to reach their audience at every stage of their journey. Right from establishing domain expertise through whitepapers and case study downloads, to building credibility through video ads and finally generating enquiries, LinkedIn's suite of ad formats can cater to every step of the way.

YouTube

Videos are becoming one of the most consumed forms of media on the internet and have spawned a number of social platforms dedicated solely to creating and sharing videos. But of course, none of the newer platforms can truly dismantle the OG video viewing platform: YouTube. While YouTube has been around since 2005, its relevance and popularity has been skyrocketing in recent years. In India, over 250 million users watch YouTube videos each month and this number encapsulates multiple age groups, income levels, and other demographics.

YouTube's growing viewer base has made it one of the most effective platforms to advertise on. YouTube ads have a viewability rate of 95 percent while 7 out of 10 viewers watch the ads with the sound on. This points towards a highly-engaged audience that brands would do well to tap into. YouTube provides a variety of different ad formats that brands can choose from depending upon their objective and budgets. TrueView instream ads are skippable after 5 seconds, while Bumper ads are 6 seconds long and cannot be skipped. Brands can also advertise on the YouTube search results page, the homepage or on the video view page.

YouTube is also a platform best used for creating awareness of a certain product or brand. While it can certainly drive enquiries and leads, it's most effective when you use it to create a compelling story around your brand and use that to create a closer connection with your audience.

Google Search

For all intents and purposes, Google is practically every user's go-to search engine. Regardless of who your audience is, chances are, they are actively searching for something on Google at least a few times a day. But Google's biggest strength is not that it has arguably the biggest audience base in the world, but that its audience approaches it with a very high intent. A user looking for a

'2-bedroom apartment in North Bangalore' is actively in the market for one. If you are able to showcase your ad to this user, chances are you're looking at gaining a very qualified lead.

If your product has a very direct selling point and can fulfill a user's immediate need, then Google Search is one of the best platforms to advertise on. The key to succeeding on Search is to bid on the right keywords and craft compelling ad copies. The keywords that you bid on need to be directly related to your product offering and have a sizable monthly search volume to increase the number of impressions your ad gets. But even if your product can fulfill a user's need, they might not recognize that unless you write ad copies that capture this. If you nail both these points, you can expect your ads on Google Search to give you a good number of conversions.

Google Display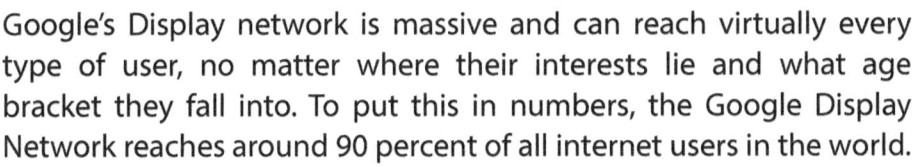

Google's Display network is massive and can reach virtually every type of user, no matter where their interests lie and what age bracket they fall into. To put this in numbers, the Google Display Network reaches around 90 percent of all internet users in the world. That is a huge audience for you to tap into.

However, the downside to advertising on Google Display is that most users are not actively looking to fulfill a need, the way they are on Google Search. Users are primarily exploring their websites of interest and might not be willing to leave it by clicking on a website ad. Because of this, conversions and lead quality through Display tend to be significantly lower than Google Search. But does this mean you shouldn't invest in Display at all? Not necessarily! Display can be a powerful way to continue building awareness among users, retarget them and slowly influence their purchase decision. So while your display ads might not be contributing directly to leads, they could be a very important indirect influence.

The digital universe is so wide and varied that no matter what segment your brand falls into, you can easily find the right audience. The deciding factor in the success of your ads will ultimately depend upon the digital marketing mix you determine, based on your unique objectives and available resources.

CHAPTER 12

Building Coalitions and Advocates: The Power of Influencer Marketing

Baboon troops are some of the most stratified and rigid social structures found anywhere in the world, natural or man-made. At its head is the alpha male, who has first rights over resources. But despite being the strongest member of the troop, the alpha's position is tenuous. At any moment, an ambitious juvenile baboon can increase his sphere of influence by appealing to other members to join his coalition. With his new supporters behind him, he can now overpower and overthrow the erstwhile alpha.

Oftentimes the best way to beat the competition is to form strategic coalitions with a certain type of individual who has a devoted base: an influencer. A stamp of approval from an influencer known for their good taste can make or break a brand.

Technically, influencers are hardly a recent phenomenon. For centuries, human beings have always looked up to certain individuals who they perceive as being the 'gold standard' in society. They look up to them for advice on how to act, what to wear, what to buy and where to go. Chances are, you've followed the advice of an influencer within your circle, however unwittingly. Just think back to the last time you wanted to buy a phone or a laptop and who helped you make that decision.

What stands out about influencers in the modern age is the sheer scale they can operate on. Influencers in the offline world have a limited scope of, well, influence. A tech-savvy friend might be able to share recommendations with a few of his/her close contacts, but that's as much as they can do. Additionally, the gates to becoming a large-scale influencer were open to only a limited few. Celebrities and TV hosts were possibly the only types of influencers who had a large reach.

Today, however, anyone can create a social media account, post regularly and, if their content is worth it, gain a massive following. You don't have to struggle for years or get a lucky break to achieve influencer status; you just need a good internet connection. The ease of taking your talent to the internet has led to an explosion of influencers in virtually every category. On a broad level, there are influencers in the field of fashion, beauty, lifestyle, automobiles, etc. But what's really interesting is that there are influencers (with dedicated followings) in extremely niche spaces. For instance, 'bookstagram' and 'booktube' have become huge in recent years. Dig in a little deeper into this niche and you'll find separate influencer circles around fantasy fiction, YA fiction and so on. Similarly, within the larger 'health' influencer category are a set of niche subcategories like 'vegan', 'raw vegan', 'fruitarian', and so on.

So why should your brand care about diving into the endless rabbithole of influencer categories? Because somewhere within that lies a group of individuals who are your exact TA and need only the recommendation of their influencer in order to try out your product.

The Undeniable Importance of Influencer Marketing

In simple terms, influence marketing produces very real business results. In one survey, around 34% of Instagram users bought a product because an influencer they followed recommended it. Influencers can often be more effective than huge celebrities when it comes to shaping buying decisions. This can be traced back to the personal touch that marks influencer interactions. Unlike celebrities, who are seen as an unattainable ideal, influencers are far more relatable. They share personal aspects of their lives with their followers, offer in-depth tutorials on how to achieve their looks, reveal all the products they use and aren't afraid to bare their souls to their followers. Unlike celebrities, whose lives are shrouded in mystery, influencers are only too happy to fling open their doors to the world and give them behind the scenes access.

This openness shapes their interactions and influence over their followers to a huge extent. Their followers are a lot more likely to connect with them on a personal level and thus, believe in their recommendations. If your brand or product is recommended by an influencer, you immediately gain visibility and credibility in their eyes of their followers. This awareness very often translates to sales, thus making influencer marketing one of the best marketing strategies for high ROI.

Case Study: How we increased brand awareness and engagement on Instagram for Tata CLiQ

Industry: E-commerce

Objective: To increase engagement on Tata CLiQ's Instagram handle and improve positive engagement at the same time

Strategy: This requirement was pretty straightforward and got us thinking, who are actually the followers of Tata CLiQ and what do they miss the most? The users of Tata CLiQ are shopaholics who miss shopping and hanging out with their friends at the mall due to the ongoing lockdown. The solution was to bring back the malls itself! So what if people can't visit the mall, we can bring the mall to their fingertips.

Thus, we had a BIG idea, a virtual mall. A chance for the audience to live the nostalgia from the comfort of the couch. Visiting a mall was now just a click away, and thus emerged #MallAtACLiQ. We made a virtual mall on Tata CLiQ's Instagram handle with all the offline mall experiences of shopping, gaming, food, clubbing and fun. This idea was true to the whole purpose of e-commerce i.e. bringing the malls on people's palms.

We created a 4 storey mall interior on Tata CLiQ's Instagram timeline with each floor having multiple shops. Each shop had a host in the form of an influencer who guided the user in terms of styling. We chose 4 influencers to host the audience at our virtual mall and help them decide on their choices of shoes, clothing, watches and jewellery via a lookbook video. This activity helped us deliver a more personalised experience to our Instagram audience.

Since the objective also aimed at improving positive engagement, we laced our 4 storey grid with contests and engaging content on every floor. These content enabled scores of users to turn up and engage with our posts therefore lifting the engagement rate for our Instagram handle.

We also tied up with a social discovery channel partner in order to boost our reach. The campaign was well received and appreciated by the audience there. This not only multiplied our reach capabilities but also improved the authenticity of our message, giving proof of the idea being accepted by all.

Business Impact:

The video along with the static posts was promoted on Instagram to a pan-India working-class audience for more engagement and reach using Facebook's RnF buying technique.

- 20 million+ reach for our campaign
- 26 million+ impressions
- 2.4 million+ engagements

How to Zero in on the Best Influencers for Your Brand

While influencer marketing can be one of the most cost-effective marketing strategies, it isn't as simple as finding the most popular influencers and then partnering with them. In reality, influencer marketing isn't always about how popular your influencers are, but how appropriate they are. Do they have the audience that will be most likely to purchase your product? Does their aesthetic and content format align with yours?

Here are some of the most important factors that you should take into consideration when choosing the best influencers to partner with.

1. Do Your Background Research

Partnering with the wrong type of influencer can have disastrous consequences for your brand, both from a sales and a brand perception point of view. For instance, if your brand has strong conservative values and your influencer's social media presence is anything but, this could cause a strong dissonance. To avoid this, do your research into an influencer's history, dive deep into their posts and check the kind of content they post about. Only when you are certain that they align with your brand image should you consider partnering with them.

2. Check their Social Metrics

Brands often go by the number of followers an influencer has as a way to decide whether they should collaborate with the influencer. However, phenomena like fake followers and followers exchanges can inflate this number, making it unreliable. You want to partner with an influencer who has a genuinely invested audience. To determine this, you should check two metrics: Reach and Engagement. Reach will tell you how many individuals can view their posts on an average while Engagement will tell you how many of their followers actively engage with their content. The latter is extremely important to help you determine the quality of their followers.

3. Demographics of their Audience

When you have a clear insight into who your target audience is, you need to ensure that there is a sufficient overlap with your influencer's audience as well. This is extremely important because even if you get a lot of views and engagement on the sponsored post, this won't translate into sales unless the audience is relevant. For instance, you could be selling products only within Mumbai, but your influencer's audience is primarily from Delhi. Or, even more commonly, your TA might be in tier 2 cities, while your influencer's audience is largely limited to urban cities. Doing a complete analysis in advance can help you ensure your post is reaching the right audience.

4. Scale of the Influencer

Most brands want to partner with the biggest influencer within their budget to get the maximum reach. However, this might not always be the most effective option. Research has shown that micro-influencers (influencers with followers between 1000–1,00,000) often have a more dedicated following and their audience is more likely to trust their recommendations. In fact, studies have also shown that when influencers gain more followers, their average engagement rate steadily drops. Thus, you should definitely consider partnering with micro-influencers, especially if you have a limited budget or offer a niche product.

5. Platforms Leveraged by the Influencer

While many influencers are active on most social media platforms, almost all of them have one specific platform they are strongest in and have the most engagement on. For example, the primary platform for an influencer could be Instagram, YouTube, Facebook,

LinkedIn or an independent blog. With the rise of new vernacular platforms geared towards tier 2 audiences, the primary platform could even be Trell, Roposo, Chingari, etc. You need to make sure that their primary platform is streamlined with the audience for your own brand. For example, if you have a business product, you should find influencers popular on LinkedIn. If you want to showcase a makeup product, then you can find influencers on YouTube who can use it for a makeup tutorial.

Influencer marketing is fast emerging as one of the most bankable marketing strategies a brand can adopt. There are numerous brands like Colourpop who have become massive solely through influencers. Once you identify the right influencers and they help widen your brand's reach, the sky's the limit!

Lower Funnel: Going the Extra Mile to Convert Potential Customers into a Loyal Customer, and Driving ROI to Meet Your Goals

Should humans be defined by their mere internet search behaviour as spelled out by conventional marketing theories? How can your brand understand the real intent of customers, respond appropriately and drive them to convert?

CHAPTER 13

Responding to Signals: Intent-Based Targeting

One of the most awe-inspiring sounds of the Serengeti is the majestic roar of the lion – a sound that can travel over 7 kilometres. Lion roars might sound the same to us, but for fellow lions, they're a very clear sign of communication. Lions clearly communicate intent through their roars, whether it's a warning sign to potential intruders or friendly calls to other members of the coalition. Other lions in the area can then choose how to respond to these roars after deciphering their true intent.

Many of us tend to think of our audience as homogeneous groups. But modern audiences are fluid and can be hard to accurately define through objective parameters. Instead, what pays is to understand their real intent and respond accordingly.

A fair amount of the groundwork done to get the scoop on your target audience focuses on objective demographic data and in some cases, psychographic data. Typically, you might think of your targeting along the lines of: 45-year old homemaker in an urban city who enjoys shopping and is health-conscious. While this data might tell you what your ideal customer looks like, it makes a dangerous assumption: that human beings can be fit into tightly-defined pigeonholes.

Forget about marketing theories for a moment and think back to your own interests and behaviour on the internet. At the start of the week, you might have been motivated to revamp your lifestyle and make healthier life choices. You search for yoga mats, organic snack foods, workout clothes and herbal teas. Your search behaviour immediately puts you into a 'health and fitness category' and the ad targeting begins. But a few days in, you crave for something indulgent and start searching for recipes and ingredients for a sinfully rich chocolate cake. You also decide to treat yourself to a nice meal out and you start searching for restaurants near you. Lo and behold, you now find yourself in the 'foodies' category. Also imagine that you are 65 years old; an age bracket that many brands generally do not target for health, fitness or food. You might well be the exact customer they're looking for, but because you don't match their predefined targeting, you will most likely never see their ads.

The simple truth is that human beings are unique, wildly different and rarely consistent creatures. Conventional targeting parameters are rarely sufficient to cover the exact target audience a brand should focus on. These demographic targeting details are sometimes seen as a hangover from the age of traditional data-starved forms of advertising. While these metrics serve offline forms of marketing perfectly well, online media offers a range of granular data that outperform demographic details.

The digital space offers brands the opportunity to target audiences not on their objective characteristics, but on their *intent*. It doesn't matter if you're male or female, young or old, if you exhibit behaviour that indicates you might be interested in a specific product or service, a relevant brand can target you.

There are a number of ways to identify intent and target audiences and these techniques vary depending upon the platform you choose. In this chapter, we have broken down the different types of intent-based targeting on platforms like Facebook, Google and YouTube.

Facebook

Facebook is one of the most widely-used platforms in the world and is one of the only platforms which has users across a range of demographics. Because of this, Facebook has a wealth of data-backed targeting options that can help you zero in on your exact target audience.

Behavioural Targeting

Behavioural targeting helps you identify users based on certain actions they have taken on Facebook. These options can help you find extremely niche audiences and thus improve conversions on your ads.

Some of the behavioural targeting options on Facebook are:

- Life events (eg. anniversary coming up in XX days, recently engaged, recently married, in a new relationship, birthday coming up in XX days, etc.)
- Parents (eg. new parents, parents of toddlers, parents of preschoolers, parents with teenagers, etc.)
- Interests (eg. business, movies, entertainment, fashion, music, gaming, etc.)
- Browser type (eg. Chrome, Safari, etc.)
- Mobile device (eg. iPhone users, Android users, specific mobile phone models)
- Job role (eg. advertising executive, accountant, sales, etc.)

These are just a sample of the multitude of targeting options available on Facebook. The flipside of the variety of options available is that you need an in-depth, intimate understanding of your audience in order to identify the most accurate options for your product or brand. As long as your first-level of consumer research is bang on target, Facebook's range of behavioural targeting options can help you identify the best mix of audiences who are the most likely to engage or convert.

Custom Audiences

Custom audiences are audiences that have previously engaged with your brand in some shape or form. This is a powerful targeting tool because you are able to display your ads to people who already know about your brand and have expressed interest in it in the past. These groups of people are most likely to convert quickly as they are past the awareness stage. Custom audiences will also play a huge role in your customer retention strategy and in encouraging brand loyalty.

Based on the type of engagement, there are specific custom audiences you can build:

- **Website visitors:** Website visits are an important interest signal because it means that these users were interested enough in your product to visit your website and learn more about it. Once you add the Facebook Pixel on your website, Facebook will be able to track users who visit your website and allow you to target them on Facebook.

- **Lead form audiences:** You can use this option to either target users who have enquired but not converted, or who have enquired in previous campaigns. This, again is an important signal or a user's interest in your brand or product.

- **Video view:** If you have run video campaigns, you can target users who viewed those videos. This is an important targeting option in a full-funnel marketing strategy as you can use videos to create awareness and then target users who viewed them with more targeted communication to push them towards a conversion.

- **Engagement audiences:** Engagement audiences are users who have engaged with your brand's social media assets across Facebook and Instagram. An interesting feature about engagement audiences is that you can set a time range for the data, so you can keep the targeting as fresh and relevant as you need to.

Once you have this data through Custom Audiences, you can even target segments of users within each audience for greater accuracy and personalization.

Lookalike Audiences

Lookalike audiences are a powerful targeting option because they help you reach audiences that are very likely to convert and that you might not have been able to identify otherwise.

Lookalike audiences are audiences which are similar to your custom audiences. For instance, you might have a database of 500 users who have visited your website and these constitute a highly-relevant section of your target audience. But, obviously, these 500 users are not enough to scale up sales on your website. In this case, you can create a 'lookalike audience' of the 500 users and tap into a larger database of users who share several similar traits to your original custom audience. Facebook's algorithm will identify key traits of your custom audience (such as their age, gender, behaviour, etc.) and find users who closely match these same traits. You can also control the size of your lookalike audience. The smaller your lookalike, the more closely they resemble your original database. As you increase the size, the identification parameters become less tightly defined.

Google Search

Of all the forms of intent-based targeting, Google Search is possibly the most reliable way to identify and target users based on their intent. This is because keywords themselves indicate intent. If I search for 'women's black running shoes', I'm a potential customer for a sports shoe brand, regardless of my age, gender or other demographic markers. To ensure that your targeting is even more accurate, Google also allows you to layer audience targeting options on Google search ads. This helps you serve up ads that are more personalized and can guarantee you higher returns on your investment.

You have a few main options when it comes to targeting users on Google Search.

RLSA

Remarketing Lists for Search Ads allows you to target users who have already visited your website. If they have already done some level of research on your brand, then they just need a final push towards making a conversion. In these cases, you can offer those users promotional discounts or coupons to convince them to convert. Users who haven't visited your website, on the other hand, will be shown a more generic ad copy, around your brand's USPs or products. This helps you leverage the full-funnel approach on Google Search.

In-Market Audiences

In-market audiences, as the name suggests, are audiences who are 'in the market' to purchase a specific product or service. Since these users have already identified a need and are doing their research to find the best brand for their requirements, showcasing the right ad message to them can convince them to purchase from your brand. You can choose from a huge variety of in-market audiences, based on what product or service you offer. For example, you can choose audiences who are in the market to purchase sports shoes, a new laptop, a new house, and much more.

Demographics

Just as with Facebook, you can also narrow down users based on specific demographic details. This comes in useful when you have identified that certain segments of users are more likely to convert. Demographic-based targeting can also help you display personalized messages to different sets of users. For instance, an e-commerce website could display personalized messages to parents, single women, middle-aged men and so on. This kind of personalization in your ad copies can lead to higher clicks and conversions.

Similar Audiences

If you are trying to expand your existing consumer base, then Google's similar audience targeting feature will help you find the best match while broadening the pool. Once you have uploaded a remarketing list, Google will be able to identify other users who exhibit similar behaviour and thus have the highest potential of converting.

Affinity

An 'affinity' audience is one that has interests and behaviours that indicate they would be interested in a specific product category. For instance, an ideal customer for a company that makes granola bars would be one who is interested in fitness, does yoga, likes to use natural products and is interested in outdoor activities. To drill down even deeper, you can build custom affinity audiences by adding specific website URLs or interests you want to build an audience around.

Combined Audiences

To make every buck you spend on marketing count, you should use a combination of these targeting options for the most accurate audience targeting. You can, for example, layer specific keyword targeting with demographic targeting and affinity audiences to get a sizable pool of consumers that are the best fit for your product.

Google Display Network

Google's Display Network offers brands an excellent way to build top-of-the-mind recall among your audience by consistently appearing on relevant websites that they are exploring. GDN also offers an array of targeting options that can ensure you reach the right audience at the right time and place. The sheer vastness of the display network makes precise targeting all the more important to eliminate the possibility of junk leads.

There are two main ways you can target users on GDN.

Remarketing for Conversions

This is when you showcase your ads to users who have already visited your website. Your display ads will be shown to them on the various websites they travel to help re-engage with them and push them closer towards making a conversion.

Prospecting for Brand Awareness

You can reach new audiences through the various audience targeting options available on GDN. Similar to Google Search, you can target audiences using custom intent, custom affinity and demographic filters. You can also narrow down a list of websites where your target audience is more likely to be exploring and choose to display your ads on those.

YouTube

YouTube is quickly becoming a key ingredient in every brand's marketing mix and for good reason. This platform is hugely popular across age groups and demographics. The nature of the platform also means you can be more creative with your ads and produce campaigns that deliver better results.

On YouTube, there are three broad forms of targeting that can help you reach the right audience.

Custom Intent and Affinity

You can build custom intent (audiences who have the intention to purchase a product or service) and custom affinity audiences

(audiences who have the likelihood of being interested in your product or service based on their internet behaviour) on YouTube. These audiences on YouTube are built based on search terms audiences have used on Google and YouTube. Unlike display targeting, intent-based targeting on YouTube does not access user's behaviour on other websites through cookie data.

Video Remarketing

Video remarketing is an excellent way to reacher viewers who have already expressed some form of interest in your brand or are already aware of it. Through remarketing, you can specifically target users who have subscribed to your channel, watched videos from your channel or even watched a specific video. This helps you get maximum ROI on your marketing spends.

Video Sequencing

Video sequencing is a powerful strategy brands can deploy as part of their full-funnel marketing strategy. This technique allows brands to control exactly what order in which users are exposed to their video ads. For example, video 1 that a user views can be general USPs of the product the brand offers to create awareness and video 2 can be more targeted information about special offers and how to buy the product to convert the user.

Programmatic Advertising

Programmatic advertising is quickly becoming the biggest marketing trend of the decade. Google predicted that by the end of 2019, around 60 percent of all ad budgets would be directed towards programmatic. The push for programmatic advertising is in line with the greater demand for automation and higher ROI on marketing budgets coming in from every corner. Programmatic advertising is an automated process of real-time bidding on ad inventory. It allows you to target specific websites that your audience is active on, set your targeting parameters through DV360 or use first-party data.

Through programmatic advertising, brands can gain and leverage huge volumes of data; this can be split into first-party data (data provided by the company itself), second-party data (provided by an advertising agency) and third-party data (which can be purchased from a company). Based on the insights drawn from this data, programmatic ads can be precisely targeted for maximum results.

Intent-based targeting is a new format of audience profiling and targeting built exclusively for the digital age. It provides brands with unprecedented control over who sees their ads, how many times and at precisely what moment in their purchase journey.

Chapter 14

Hidden Sanctuaries: Emerging Digital Ecosystems

The Serengeti can give a visitor a false sense of endlessness, but like most other resources, it is finite – and increasingly fragile. Environmental and manmade pressures on the grasslands have threatened to disrupt the delicate ecosystem and the very existence of the animals which call these grasslands home. This has led to several protected sanctuaries sprouting up within the Serengeti. Inside the fences of these sanctuaries, animals can grow and thrive, closed off from threats.

The internet is often described as an infinite interconnected web where everything can be tracked and targeted. But within this web are independent walled gardens where users momentarily step off the main grid and into whole new digital 'sanctuaries'.

The 'internet' in the sense that most of us think about is an all-pervasive universe, synonymous with the 'world wide web'. As advertisers, with the right targeting and the right budgets, we can reach our audience no matter where they step in this universe. But ever so often, our audience steps away from this open playground and into a protected walled garden where the gates are shut to conventional methods of advertising. Social media, of course, is one of the best examples of a platform where advertising is monitored and users cannot be targeted through display or search ads. But even more closed than social media are two emerging platforms where users are spending an increasing amount of their time.

E-commerce and OTT platforms satisfy the two very basic needs of every human: to be gratified and to be entertained. With the improved ease of use and the range of options available on these platforms, the percentage of time spent on them is growing by the minute. If your marketing strategy does not extend to these platforms, then you are missing an opportunity to engage with your audience during important segments of their day.

Advertising on e-commerce and OTT requires an in-depth understanding of how users approach these platforms in the first place. In this chapter, we will be examining the growth of e-commerce and OTT in India, key players in these spaces and how these segments are expected to evolve in the coming years.

The New Digital Marketplace

If you go through your Amazon order history, you might be slightly alarmed to find out how much you actually spend in a month. In 2018, India accounted for 100 billion sessions and a massive $33 billion shopping online on Amazon. A PWC report predicted that by 2022, this number will rise to $100 billion. The ease with which we can find virtually any product, enjoy quick shipping and easy returns has turned most of us into online shopping junkies. Apart from the obvious giants like Amazon and Flipkart, India has also produced a number of homegrown platforms with niche services. Fashion, beauty, technology, art, groceries, you name it and there's an online store for it. As product ranges on these e-commerce sites increase, footfalls to physical stores are likely to drop. While this is a challenge to the stores themselves, it also poses a threat to consumer products that for long depended on physical stores to drive sales.

The strategy of marketing to a customer on a physical store versus an online store is completely different. In a physical store, a product would primarily depend upon two things to get a consumer's attention: the product packaging and its placement.

Eye-level shelves are prime property, while a floor-level shelf makes you less likely to get picked up. On online stores, however, the competition is bigger than just a few other products on different shelves. Depending on the size of the store, you could be competing against a huge array of brands spread across the country. Let's say you were shopping for women's shampoo, for example. In your local grocery store, you might have around 10 brands to compare before you finally select one. If you were to go to Amazon, you would have about 10 times that number. Standing out from the stiff competition on an online megastore is a whole different ball game. Here, it isn't just your packaging that needs to grab eyeballs, but also your product title and description. And of course, reviews are readily available on e-commerce sites so if your reviews are bad, even the best package design can't save you.

With the intense competition on e-commerce platforms, depending upon organic views alone to generate orders might not be the best route. Consumers search for products or categories on e-commerce stores with the clear intention of making a purchase. If you're losing visibility to a competitor during this critical step, this could translate into serious losses. This is where advertising on e-commerce platforms comes in. E-commerce platforms aren't just a place for you to list your products, they're an active marketplace where you can push your product to the forefront and get maximum clicks and sales from it. One of the biggest advantages of advertising on e-commerce sites is that users only come to these platforms with a clear intention of purchasing a product. When you run display ads or ads on social media for your product, you're hoping to build awareness of your product and offer users a compelling enough CTA that they abandon what they're currently doing and instead, click on your ad and buy the product. When you advertise on e-commerce platforms, however, you know for a fact that a user is already in the market to buy a certain product and if you can get their attention, then they are very likely to buy yours.

E-commerce marketing is also important because these websites and apps are quickly becoming places where people spend a chunk of their time online. Take the e-commerce giant, Amazon, for example. In just 2 weeks leading up to their annual Prime Day event, over a million Indian users shopped on the platform. But even if your customers are not always directly purchasing your product on Amazon, there's strong evidence to suggest that simply being exposed to the product on an e-commerce site can influence offline purchases. An estimated $70 billion in offline sales influenced by online research was estimated to have been generated in 2019.

One of the most effective and accurate ways to reach your target audience is through advertising on e-commerce sites. Ads help you 'skip the line' so to speak and push your products to relevant customers who are in the market for it. On Amazon, Sponsored Brand ads are extremely effective and can drive awareness of a new brand that users might not already be familiar with. Sponsored Products are similar; they display the promoted product in a very natural way within the lists of products that consumers are scrolling through.

Because Amazon sees such massive traffic from a diverse range of consumers, it also offers a variety of targeting options that can help ensure your product is seen by the right audience. For instance, you can target in-market segments (eg. customers in the market to buy a refrigerator), lifestyle segments (eg. customers who are interested in fitness and nutrition) and even set custom segments.

The Changing E-Commerce Customer

E-commerce has transformed the lives of Indian customers since its introduction, but in the next wave of growth, the new breed of customers will likely transform e-commerce in turn. Consumers from non-metro cities and towns in India are increasingly coming online and are open to transacting on e-commerce platforms, but the way they do so will be very different from the initial generation of e-commerce customers. The PWC report marks key differences in transactional behaviour of the first 50 million Indian e-commerce users and the next 100 million. The main point of difference, of course, is the language in which these customers navigate sites. The first group of e-commerce customers were largely comfortable with English and navigated through websites using typed queries. But the next 100 million users are more comfortable in their native language and might also not be used to typing on mobile phones. For them, voice search will be a key service and as a result, voice commerce as a whole is expected to explode in India over the coming years.

Another key difference is in the buying behaviour. The next 100 million e-commerce customers will most likely have a lower ticket size than the first 50 million. This is an extremely price-conscious segment and is unlikely to make very expensive purchases online. This is also partly because they might still not fully trust e-commerce platforms and are more likely to spend large amounts of money at an offline retailer they have more confidence in. Another effect of this trust deficit is the fact that these customers will prefer paying through cash-on-delivery rather than through online payment gateways.

To address these concerns, e-commerce players need to re-evaluate their website navigational flow, communicate clearly the security of their payment gateways and encourage offline modes of payment. Adapting to the needs of the new e-commerce customer might pose a few challenges, but it would be well worth the effort. As the spending power and aspirations of these customers grow, they will soon see themselves becoming the most coveted customer segment in India.

The Rise of OTT in India

Until just a few years ago, screen time usually meant gathering around the television to watch the new episode of a favourite television show. New episodes would be released daily and in some cases monthly. If the episode ended on a cliffhanger (as any good TV show worth their salt would), we would have to wait with bated breath until the next episode came out. Today, however, our definition of screen time is completely different. Most of us have made a shift from cable and DTH to a whole new viewing platform: OTT. OTT (over-the-top) media has more or less blown traditional television out of the water, offering TV shows and movies on demand. Instead of waiting patiently for new episodes to release, a new concept of 'binge watching' was born, since most shows are released in their entirety (with a few notable exceptions, of course).

The popularity of OTT is not without its challenges. According to a report by social streaming platform FLYX, India currently has one of the highest OTT subscription price as a percentage of monthly income at 2.77%. The same study showed that by comparison, USA has a percentage of 0.22% while Australia is one of the lowest at 0.15% But despite these roadblocks, OTT isn't going anywhere. As audiences move away from television channels, many networks have launched their own OTT platform in a bid to retain their viewers. And again on these platforms, it's vernacular that's leading the charge. Even among the major players in the space, the popularity of the platform appears to be dependent on the amount of regional language offerings it has. Hotstar, with the most regional content dominates with over 29% of the market share. Netflix with the least, has a little less than 5% of the market share. A number of smaller OTT platforms catered exclusively for regional audiences have started popping up too. Platforms like MX player, Balaji Alt, Zee 5 and Voot are steadily growing in popularity thanks to their regional content library and lower subscription prices.

While from a content creator's perspective, this shift to OTT viewership is definitely exciting (free from the shackles of the censor board and primetime viewing competition, there's no limit to the avenues creators can explore on OTT), but from an advertiser's perspective, this change is even more welcome. The diversity of audiences on these platforms and the increasing amount of time that viewers are spending on them points to OTT being the next big avenue for digital advertising in India. In February 2020, there were an average of 11,000 ad insertions on OTT platforms (as per data by TAM). In April 2020 – with the lockdown boosting OTT viewing ever further – the same report shows that the number of ad insertions increased to 33,000.

Hotstar, the undeniable giant in the Indian OTT space, for example, has a hugely diverse content library, which is one of the key drivers behind its growth. 40% of users on the platform consume content in languages like Bengali, Tamil, Marathi, Telugu and Malayalam. The platform's range of targeting options can help advertisers easily narrow down their audience. You can target users based on their interest, geographical location, demographics, languages spoken and even the genre watched.

Similarly, ZEE5's strength lies in the fact it has a strong, region tier-2 connect. With programming available in 12 different Indian languages and a strong penetration in non-metro cities and towns, the platform has become a force to be reckoned with within a very short period of time. ZEE5 currently boasts over 63 million monthly active users with 536 million monthly video views. Apart from the diverse audience available to advertisers to target, ZEE5 also has a host of ad formats like Display, Roadblocks and Mastheads to garner visibility for your brand.

The Road Ahead for OTT

When OTT first made their debut, they were primarily envisioned as a content viewing platform users could access on their phones or at the very most, their laptops. But as SmartTV prices keep dropping lower and devices like the Firestick can transform practically any TV into a SmartTV, a growing number of users are accessing OTT platforms on their televisions. This is by far the biggest threat to traditional TV channels. With OTT having much of the same content that television channels have with the added advantages of being on-demand, skippable and with larger content libraries, it's easy to see why users seem to be moving away from TV and towards OTT. If your current media plan budget revolves around primetime bids for TV spots and a smaller portion dedicated to digital to simply support your television campaign, it might be time to flip the table.

E-commerce and OTT platforms present an exciting opportunity for advertising to reach their audience in completely different formats. With their growing pervasiveness in every consumer's everyday life, incorporating both platforms in your marketing mix will become vital.

Chapter 15

Tracking Paw Prints in the Ground: Measuring Results from Digital

Measuring and Driving Business Results

The vast expanse of the Serengeti can make it difficult to spot the most elusive animals. Tall stalks of grass, deep muddy ponds and camouflaged animals are not your friend when you're trying to check off animals from your list. But a seasoned guide knows exactly what signs to look for. Smudged paw prints on the ground, circling vultures in the sky and warning calls from birds floating through the air can lead them straight to what they're looking for.

The best designed campaigns don't mean anything unless they translate into tangible results. But with the granularity of data digital campaigns can provide, it can become difficult to look between the stalks of grass and spot what is actually important.

Your creatives are ready, your ads are running, your blogs are live, now what? The beauty of digital marketing is that it's far from a static strategy. It can constantly be analyzed, tweaked and optimized to improve your results. But to do this effectively, you need to know what you're looking for and what you want to achieve. Digital campaigns can offer you a wealth of information, but not all of it might be aligned with your business objectives. In a situation where you go in without a compass to guide your marketing efforts, there are two outcomes that can happen: either you focus on the wrong metrics that won't translate into business results or you don't look at the performance data at all and miss out on key learning which could help your future campaigns perform better.

The guiding light which points you in the right direction and helps you ignore the clutter are your marketing KPIs. KPIs, or Key Performance Indicators, is a term that is familiar to any marketer, offline or digital. But with digital campaigns, zeroing in on the right KPIs becomes extremely critical because it can help you improve your campaigns in real time and allocate your budget wisely.

All Metrics aren't Created Equal

The wealth of information available on digital can be a boon or a bane depending upon how you use it. Once you narrow down on the KPIs that you believe have the most relevance for your business, you can track them to understand how well your digital marketing strategy is working.

But how do you identify the right KPIs?

Typically, there are two ways you can go wrong when selecting your KPIs.

Scenario #1 Your KPI Clashes with Your Business Objective

The business objectives that you set for your brand are the focal point from which each of your marketing activities flows. If your business objective is to generate sales through your digital campaigns, but you are only tracking engagement as your main KPI, it will not paint you an accurate picture of the campaign performance.

Scenario #2 Your KPI Cannot be Influenced

In some cases, you might be tracking a KPI that cannot be influenced by external factors. Take for example, a travel company whose main KPI was still the number of travel bookings made even during the COVID-19 lockdown. Your ads might be reaching the right people and have the right messaging, but because travel is shut down, people are not going to book a vacation regardless. This is not something that you can influence in anyway and should not be something you actively track during this period.

This also brings us to an important point! Your KPIs are not set in stone. The metrics that are relevant during one specific season or during one stage of your business might not be relevant for another.

So now that we know what *not* to do when choosing your KPIs, the question becomes, "How do you choose the best KPIs to track and measure?" In general, there are two broad categories of KPIs that you can and should track:

Conversion-Oriented KPIs

These are quantifiable metrics that are directly related to conversions or sales. If you run an e-commerce store, then the most obvious metric to measure would be sales generated daily, weekly and/or monthly. If you are running ads for a new real estate project that's launched, then lead form fills and site bookings would give you an indication of the efficacy of your campaigns.

Indication-Oriented KPIs

Some KPIs might not necessarily translate into monetary gains for your business, but could give you an indication of positive sentiment among your audience. If you have a blog, for example, and you're seeing an average time spent on the page of over three minutes, even though this might not directly lead to sales, it does mean that your audience is finding your content useful and is gaining awareness of your brand.

Channel-Wise Distribution of KPIs

As we've seen throughout this book, every platform serves a different purpose. The same customer can approach two different platforms with two completely different goals. For instance, she might visit your blog to learn more about the benefits of your product and then visit your ecommerce listing to purchase it. If you were to measure the performance of both platforms by the same yardstick, you would end up with extremely skewed results.

Typically, your KPI sheet would be divided by the different platforms you're tracking and the level of priority of each KPI. Your clicks on ads, for example, is an important metric to track, but might not be as critical for your business as the revenue generated from the ads. Of course, your KPIs are completely dependent upon your business objectives, so what you define as your primary, secondary and tertiary KPIs will have to be customized depending upon what you want to track.

In general, if we were to split the four most-tracked platforms, these would be the main KPIs that you would find most useful to track:

1. Social Media: Engagement, Followers, Website Clicks, Conversions (either through lead form fills or direct purchases)

2. PPC Campaigns: Cost Per Acquisition, Cost Per Click, Landing Page Visits, Impressions

3. SEO: Keyword Rankings, Click Through Rate, Non-Brand Clicks, Organic Leads

4. Content Marketing: Bounce Rate, Time Spent, Rankings, Organic Leads

Apart from these four main platforms, you might also want to track your email marketing performance and YouTube channel performance. In this case, some of the KPIs you'd want to track include:

Email Campaigns: Open Rate, Link Clicks, Website Visits

YouTube Channel: Subscriber Base, Watch Time, Link Clicks (if applicable), Card Click-Through-Rate

These KPIs also vary wildly depending upon the type of business category you fall into. An ecommerce website, for instance, would want to track cart abandonment rates, revenue generated through the website and customer lifetime value. A B2B company might want to track the number of downloads for their whitepapers and ebooks. Because of this, there can very rarely be a one-size-fits-all template. As long as you can successfully answer the question, "How will this KPI affect my business objectives?", then that metric is probably worth tracking.

Case Study: How we leveraged Video Sequencing YouTube and Google Display Ads during the IPL 2019 for boAt

Industry: Electronics

Objective: To leverage the signing of cricketers as brand ambassadors to drive an increase in brand and ad recall

Strategy: boAt had signed on eminent cricketing personalities like Shikhar Dhawan, KL Rahul and Hardik Pandya as brand ambassadors ahead of the IPL season. The audience had received these ambassadors well through previous creative communication from boAt on social media, and we looked to leverage this.

Through Video Sequencing, we retargeted the audience who had engaged with the first video in the sequence, to view the next and so on, over a period of 15 days. The videos featured the players in witty scenarios with boAt products and we directed each of the ads to the respective products' Amazon page. Similarly, we used catchy GIFs on Google Display Network to run ads optimised for maximum clicks, which also directed to the Amazon product page.

We leveraged the YouTube Trueview for Reach ad type on Youtube, with an aim to reach maximum people over the allocated period of time. Similarly, on Google Display we optimised the ads for maximum clicks, and also retargeted those who had already seen our YouTube ads.

We edited the longer videos to crisp, catchy 30 second videos optimised for YouTube, with a clear product CTA and product name details, for enhanced product recall. The targeting was focused on the top 5 cities based on past sales, which are Delhi, Mumbai, Bangalore, Hyderabad and Chennai. The placements were on popular Bollywood music channels, like T Series, Wave Music and Aditya Music. Once the awareness was created, we retargeted them on Google Display, with a Custom Affinity Audience of those Interested in boAt products.

Business Impact:

Through strategic execution, the campaign yielded outstanding results

- 44.4 million+ impressions for our videos
- 15.5% lift in product interest
- 59% decrease in cost per click
- 3.9 lakh+ clicks
- 158.7% lift in brand interest

The SMART Framework of KPIs

Once you have narrowed down the metrics that it makes the most business sense for you to track, it's time to set your goals for what you hope to achieve through your digital marketing efforts. The objective of setting a goal is that it is an impartial, accurate indicator of whether or not your campaigns were successful. For this reason, your goals cannot be ambiguous or loosely defined. "An increase in organic traffic to the website," for example can lead to a lot of confusion on how much of an increase counts as an achievement. A 2 percent increase and a 50 percent increase are both achievements if you go by this goal.

An easy way to set clear goals is to follow the tried-and-tested SMART framework.

S-Specific (clearly define what you want to achieve)

M-Measurable (ensure that it can be objectively quantified and tracked)

A-Attainable (can be reasonably achieved)

R-Relevant (should translate into business results)

T-Timebound (specific time period within which the goal is to be achieved)

Using the SMART framework, our previous goal of "An increase in organic traffic to the website", can now be rewritten as, "A 25% increase in organic traffic to the product pages within 6 months". This goal leaves no room for confusion. Each of your teams know what is expected of them and can accurately measure their progress over the next few months.

On the flipside, there's also a case where your KPIs might be *too* specific. For example, if you achieved a 24% increase in organic traffic, does that mean your SEO activities were a complete failure because they missed the target by 1%? Clearly, that shouldn't be the case. To avoid such scenarios, it's important to define acceptable limits on your KPIs. For example, while 25% might be your target, you can set a lower and upper boundary of 3% and an achievement within this range would still be considered an overall success.

Brand Lift Studies

Even the most well-intentioned KPIs might not always give you a clear picture of your campaign's effect on a user's purchase behaviour. KPIs that measure conversions on a Facebook ad will show you how many users that saw the ad purchased through the link directly. But it might not show you how many users became aware of your brand through those ads, mused over purchasing the advertised product for a couple of weeks and then did a direct search to learn more and purchase the product. A typical consumer's journey is far less linear than your KPI sheet would like it to be.

Brand lift studies, currently offered by Facebook and YouTube offer you a chance to get a closer understanding of this complex journey. These studies segregate your audience into control groups and measure the impact of your campaigns on audience perception before and after they go live. Rather than the usual metrics like clicks and impressions, the YouTube brand lift study (specifically BLS 2.0) measures brand recall, improvement in brand consideration, increase in purchase intent and overall brand awareness. This can help you understand how your video ads are actually impacting your consumer's decision making journey.

Clearly defined KPIs can be one of the most powerful ways to marshal teams around a single goal and achieve your business objectives. It is equally important, however, to consistently review your KPIs and evaluate if they are still relevant. If the COVID-19 pandemic has taught businesses anything, it's that even the best laid out plans can come crashing down due to external unanticipated factors. In situations like these, your KPIs need to evolve alongside the market so that they can continue to stay relevant and keep your teams aligned and working towards the same goals.

CHAPTER **16**

Bridging the Great Divide: Online-Offline Integration

The Western Corridor of the Serengeti is a less-visited but no less awe-striking area of the Serengeti. Arguably the most important feature of the Western Corridor is the Grumeti River, one of the two rivers wildebeest herds will have to cross during the Great Migration. Don't be fooled by the grassy riverbanks and innocuous still waters – the river is swarming with crocodiles beneath the surface. Getting from one side of the river to the other is treacherous and many can get lost in the attempt.

There is a seemingly similar unbridgeable divide between the online and the offline world. Does this mean that data from online campaigns and offline sales can get lost in this chasm? How can you tie in your digital efforts with your on-the-ground sales?

As we've stated multiple times throughout the course of the book, the digital world is trackable to the last second. Every interaction a user has with your ad or your website can be monitored. But what happens when they step out of the realm of the world wide web and into the real, far less trackable, world? Say, for example, you run an offline retail store. While you run ads on social media to attract an audience, the final purchase can only happen at a physical outlet. In this scenario, you might be getting good traction on your ads, but how can you know for sure if these clicks on your ads are actually translating into footfall to your store?

Another scenario is a common structural roadblock in most organizations: the division of the sales and marketing teams. In a real estate company, for example, the marketing team would be responsible for getting site visit bookings through their landing page. Once the lead has enquired, it now becomes the responsibility of the sales team to convert them – a process which happens offline in most cases. The sales team calls the lead, convinces them to visit the site and once they're at the site, gives them the information they need and nudges them closer towards making an investment in the property. Both the marketing and the sales team operate in silos, with neither having a complete picture of the entire customer journey from the online world to the offline one.

Fortunately, digital marketing and analytics have evolved to make offline tracking possible as well. Using the right tools, you can get a reasonably accurate picture of just how many actual offline visits results from your digital campaigns.

There are two main ways to track offline metrics: through Facebook and through Google. In this chapter, we will breakdown how to enable offline tracking on both platforms and how to get the most out of your ads.

Offline Events on Facebook

Regardless of where you are located, what your budget is or who your audience is, the first step of setting up a Facebook campaign is universal: You need to set your objective. Most of the objectives are related to online events like reach, traffic and engagement. If your objective is an offline conversion, then these objectives will clearly not apply to you. Instead, you can choose the 'Store Visits' objective to ensure that Facebook optimizes for it. When you choose this objective, Facebook allows you to select the stores you want to drive visits to (if you have more than one), target the people living in the immediate vicinity of the store, and even create dynamic local ads. These ads will customize the locality, store name, pin code and directions depending upon what location the user is viewing the ad from. You can also choose among a range of offline events CTAs like 'Call Now', 'Message', and 'Get Directions'. Depending upon your main objective, you can choose the CTA that makes the most sense for you. If you want to drive in-store customers for your retail outlet, then 'Get Directions' will be the most relevant, however if you are a restaurant looking to increase reservations, then 'Call Now' might be the most appropriate.

Once you have set up your ads and your campaign is live, Facebook will then use a combination of GPS tracking data and Facebook check-in data to extrapolate how many physical store visits your ads were able to deliver. There are, of course, certain limitations to this feature and it cannot be completely accurate. For example, if your store is located in a very busy area, even though Facebook tries to filter out people who pass by your store without stepping in, this mechanism might not be fully effective. Your store visits data might be higher than the actual footfall you saw. Another scenario is when your map location is not precise. If your map location is wrongly picking up some other spot, your store visits data will not pain an accurate picture.

Since there are multiple factors to take into consideration when tracking store visits, Facebook uses modelling to estimate the store visits from a specific campaign. These modelled results are more accurate when the data set is higher, usually above 100 store visits. But even then, you cannot fully interpret 150 store visits as per Facebook as 150 actual visits to your store from your campaigns. However, these numbers can give you a good overview of how effective your ads were in driving offline purchases.

Offline customer data can also be used the other way around to improve the performance of your ads. If you have a sizable database of customers who have visited your store, then you can upload it to Facebook and use this data to improve your ads targeting. You could, for instance, retarget the same customers to encourage them to visit your store again if you're running a sale or have a new product launch. You could also create a lookalike audience from the database and increase the reach of your ads. Both of these in turn will help increase offline store visits.

Case Study: How We Won the Hearts of Brides of India through Full Funnel Marketing Campaign

Industry: Jewellery

Objective: To enable the brand's Brides of India campaign breakthrough the digital hemisphere and make it relevant for the new age brides-to-be, who are active on digital platforms through identifying and leveraging the strengths of various digital platforms starting from Search to Facebook to Instagram

Strategy: We at Social Beat leveraged the wide array of creative assets that were available for the campaign and used them in a way that would best fit digital platforms

We used YouTube in-stream ads that were targeted to 5–10 km radius to the Malabar Gold store in various cities that helped in generating store visits. The audience who watched the TVC was then retargeted using regional specific ads through display ads which also garnered store visits.

Once the awareness was created we used lead generation and store visits ads through Facebook. We leveraged Facebook's ability to showcase multiple creative formats and showed region-specific creatives via a combination of slideshow, carousels and static ads.

Instagram's ability to showcase content in a magazine layout was also leveraged to create region-specific look books for the bevvy of brides in India.

Staying in constant touch with our audience through various platforms led to the generation of greater number of leads and improved store visits in a cost-effective manner.

> **Business Impact:**
>
> This turned out to be one of the most cost-effective digital campaigns done by the brand
>
> - 1000s of store visits
> - ₹66 per cost visit

Google Local Campaigns

Undeniably, the biggest advantage of advertising on Google is the absolute behemoth it has become. In many ways, Google *is* the internet. While this has understandably raised several concerns about its growing monopoly, one of the benefits that it does offer advertisers is that it can track virtually every event, online or offline, that your audience completes. But why is advertising on Google important if you can sell products through your physical retail store? Research has shown that while 91 percent of users research a product online before buying it, 92 percent of total shopping spends is still done at offline stores. And as it turns out, Google is the main resource shoppers turn to for information before purchasing a product offline.

But while this means that running ads on Google's network and bumping up your SEO game are vital, retailers might still be concerned that there's a blindspot when it comes to understanding how well these online activities have translated into actual store visits. This is where Google's Local Campaigns come to the rescue.

Local campaigns work in two phases: first you can set up a boundary around your store – known as a geo-fence- to target users. A geofence is a predefined radius around your store (you can customize the radius). Through GPS tracking, Google will know when a user has entered the specified area and will then start displaying your ads to them. Through Google's extensive network, users can see the ads on Search, Display, YouTube or Maps. In the second phase, Google uses device tracking to report how many users who were exposed to your ad actually visited your store.

Another feature of Google ads geared towards driving and tracking offline visits is Location Extensions. Location Extensions are features that can be added to your ads which gives users the option to either get directions, call the store, get the store's address or find out the distance from their current location to the store. Since every click on these extensions is tracked, it gives you a good idea of how effective your ads are in urging users to make an offline visit.

Store visit conversions are the final reporting metric that can help you quantify how many physical store visits resulted from your campaigns. The final number of store visits that are reported by Google consists of two parts: users who were signed in at the time of visiting the store who were accurately tracked and users who were not signed in but displayed similar behaviour, leading to the safe assumption that they too visited the store after being exposed to a relevant ad. The most powerful feature of store visit conversions isn't just the final total number, but the granularity of data which can be obtained. You can, for example, pinpoint exactly which ad, which copy and which customer segment generated in the most store visits. This can help you optimize your campaigns in real time and achieve a higher ROI for every campaign.

Online purchases are certainly on the rise – with the COVID-19 pandemic accelerating this trend even further – but for the majority of businesses, brick and mortar stores are still their main point of conversion. For a long time, there remained an inescapable lacuna around online promotional activities and offline sales. However, advancements in offline tracking features are bridging this gap and helping you gain a complete view into a customer's entire journey.

Chapter 17

Getting to the Source: Choosing the Right Attribution Models

Ecosystems are complex, delicate mechanisms that we still do not completely understand. Every year during the wildebeest migration, massive herds attempt to cross the Mara river but thousands will never make it to the other side – either due to drowning or hungry crocodiles. But far from being a scene of senseless violence, this graphic event is actually crucial for the wellbeing of the entire river ecosystem. Every creature in the river, from the crocodiles and hippos to the tiniest fish is nourished by the wildebeest massacre. Thus, if you had to find the true source of the thriving river ecosystems, you would have to look away from the aquatic creatures and instead to the terrestrial wildebeest.

Accurate attribution isn't always immediately apparent at first glance. Digital marketing is a continuous cycle of launching a campaign, gaining insights and further optimizing the campaign for better performance. But with so many digital activities running concurrently, how do you attribute the true factor responsible for the ultimate results?

In a perfect world, a consumer would look at your ad, click on it and buy your product. You would know exactly what you had to spend to get the user to convert and exactly which ad to attribute the purchase to. However, as we now know, a customer's journey is far from a linear, simple journey. Your user will typically have multiple touchpoints over the course of a certain time period before they decide to finally make a purchase (or take any other action that you have qualified as a conversion). In fact, if you're doing your marketing right, this is precisely how a user *should* be exposed to your product or brand. But despite most advertisers knowing the importance of having a multi-channel approach, most attribution is still calculated based on the last click. 'Attribution' is simply the process of assigning a certain weightage to a specific platform for its contribution to driving the user towards a conversion. The default attribution model used by most marketers remains a single-touch attribution – attributing credit to only one touchpoint in a user's journey.

In 'last-click attribution', credit is simply attributed to the last touchpoint a user engaged with before converting. Thus, even if a user was repeatedly exposed to your ad on Facebook, YouTube and Display ads, but only clicked on your Search ad, the Search ad they click on alone will be attributed as the reason behind their conversion. One of the reasons for the widespread usage of the last-click attribution model is its convenience. Platforms like Facebook and Google by default report last-click results. Your Facebook ad, for example, will measure conversions for a certain ad as the number of people who completed a specified action on that ad, without taking into account the range of ads they were exposed to before that.

On the other end of the spectrum, some marketers might be tracking first-click attribution alone. In this model, conversion is attributed completely to the first touchpoint a consumer had with the product. This is based on the assumption that the first touchpoint was the most critical in creating awareness and thus the platform that contributed to the most is the most profitable to invest in.

Last-click and first-click attribution might be convenient, but in most cases, they're completely inaccurate. If you are calculating performance in this way, you might be missing out on a huge chunk of your user's journey and could also be forgoing some valuable insights which could increase your marketing ROI. Of late, with a great availability of data, a second category of attribution has emerged: multi-touch attribution. Under this category, various touchpoints in the customer's journey are accounted for and credited. A number of different multi-touch attribution models have emerged, varying on the extent to which they give weightage to different touchpoints. In this chapter, we will be exploring alternative attribution models and understanding the advantages and disadvantages each have to offer.

1. Linear Attribution

In this model, every touchpoint is given equal weightage. Thus, if a user saw your ad on Facebook, YouTube, on the Google Display Network and then finally clicked on a Google Search ad, each of these will be given an equal percentage.

While this type of attribution model does help you understand and credit the entire user journey, it is usually best suited for categories with a short lead time. For categories where the lead time is typically longer (usually in research-driven, high-investment categories), a user will have a higher number of touchpoints before finally converting. In this case, if you were to assign equal attribution to each, individual platforms would have a negligible percentage of attribution and you would be unable to understand which one was the most effective. The linear attribution model also does not take into consideration the fact that some platforms or certain ads might have a higher influence on a consumer's decision than others.

2. Time Decay Attribution

In the time decay attribution model, weightage is given in an ascending order, with the least attribution given to the first touchpoint and the most to the last touchpoint. This model is based on the assumption that the touchpoints closer to the point of conversion have a greater influence on a customer's decision than the earlier ones. So if your customer saw ads on Facebook, YouTube, Display and Search in that order, Facebook would get the least attribution, YouTube and Display would have successively higher attribution and Search would have the highest.

This type of attribution is ideal for categories which typically have multiple touchpoints because it takes into account that not each of them have equal influence. Analysis of attribution through this model can help you understand which platforms are contributing the most to conversions. However, the drawback to this model is that it can downplay the importance of the first few touchpoints, which can be an important source of discovery. If you were to minimize your Facebook ad spends based on insights from this attribution model, you might not be building awareness among your audience, which can translate to fewer conversions.

3. U-Shaped Attribution

The U-shaped attribution model is a position-based model that is sort of an amalgamation of the first-click model and the last-click model. In this model, the greatest credit is given to the first and the last touchpoint. Touchpoints in between are given equal weightage.

The advantage of this model is that it helps you get an idea of which platform contributed most to discovery and which one contributed the most to final conversions. This can help you allocate spends to a fairly accurate degree. The only con to this model is that it might not fairly represent the role platforms in between played in nurturing the user till they converted.

4. W-Shaped Attribution

The W-shaped attribution model is another position-based model and it aims to remedy the flaw in the U-shaped model. Here, equal credit is given to the first-click, the last-click and the touchpoint in the middle when the user becomes a lead. For instance, a user might have first clicked on your Search ad, filled out a download form for an e-book and officially become a lead, and finally submitted a lead form on your website, which you are tracking as a conversion. In this situation, these three key touch points will be given the highest equal attribution while all other touchpoints in between are given the remaining equally.

This attribution model helps you understand the key moments in your user's journey that influenced their decision. It can give you insight into what marketing activities paid off the most and which ones to focus most of your efforts on. There are two potential drawbacks of the W-shaped attribution model, however. If you have a very short lead cycle, you might not have enough of touchpoints to provide an accurate representation. In some cases, a lead might not always be the best predictor of conversions for you. For instance, if you see that 90 percent of leads through ebook downloads never convert and that most of your conversions happen through other sources, it might not be accurate to give it equal importance.

Data-Driven Attribution

In some cases, none of these attribution models might seem suited to you. Typically, for companies whose lead cycles are extremely long and complex, there is no clear pre-set model of attribution that accurately defines your customer's journey. Each touchpoint influences customers in a different way and none can be entirely discounted in their final decision.

Data-driven attribution is a custom attribution model that uses machine learning to analyse a user's exposure and engagement with different touchpoints and infer how it influenced their decision. One of the key ways in which the data-driven attribution (DDA) model differs from other 'rule-based' models is that it doesn't only take conversion as the end-goal to measure touch points against. In the DDA model, apart from touchpoints which directly led to a conversion, even touchpoints which might not have converted a user, but increase the possibility of them converting are taken into account. For instance, an explainer video might not have prompted a user to fill out a lead form, but it increased their trust in the product, which led to a lead form down the line.

If data-driven attribution sounds complex, that's because it is. Huge volumes of data need to be cumulated and organized in order to draw accurate inferences. This is where marketing automation becomes crucial. An automated platform which can track every step of your user's journey and calculate its efficacy can help you develop more robust marketing strategies and boost the ROI of your campaigns. While they might be a little tricker to implement, DDA models are undoubtedly the most customized and accurate way to gain a holistic view into your marketing campaigns and understand how your unique customers behave.

Which Attribution Model Should You Choose?

There's no 'best' attribution model that you can blindly select and measure up your marketing activities against. Each sector and each brand have a unique customer journey and business priorities. For example, a B2B company with a long lead cycle, large audience and multiple touchpoints might need a customized data-driven attribution model, while a smaller retailer with a limited audience might find more use from a U-shaped model. In fact, for a smaller company, a DDA model might actually end up not being of much use because there is simply not enough data to build a model on.

To choose the right attribution model, you need to clearly outline your goals from marketing and identify which metrics are the most critical for you. For example if you are a new brand looking to reach a larger audience, first-click attribution might be the most relevant for you because you are primarily concerned with building awareness. If you have a long lead cycle and lead nurturing plays a very important role for you in driving the final conversion, a position-based attribution model or a data-driven attribution model might make the most sense.

Attributing each touchpoint of your customer's journey is critical to understanding exactly how your marketing efforts have played out. Analysis with the most appropriate type of attribution model can help you gain a clearer insight into your customer behaviour, allocate ad spends more efficiently and improve results from your campaigns.

CHAPTER **18**

Artificial Intelligence and Marketing Automation

Few job markets are in a constant state of flux the way digital marketing is. The skills that you prize as a digital marketer today may be redundant tomorrow. What does the future hold for digital marketing and how do human marketers fit in?

From the get-go, one of the biggest advantages that digital marketing held over traditional marketing is the volumes of data it offered. A marketer can track virtually every step of their consumer's journey, from the exact sequence of ads they were exposed to before deciding to make a purchase, to the time of day that their ads get the most traction, to even specific interest and affinities a bulk of their consumers have. In today's hyper-connected world, data can be the most powerful asset a brand holds.

Why?

To answer that question, we need to delve into the second reason why digital marketing often bags bragging rights over traditional marketing: greater accuracy. The granularity of data available in digital marketing ensures that marketers have greater control over who views their ads and at what stage. But greater accuracy doesn't always mean complete accuracy. Digital marketers are, after all, only human and the volumes of data they have to deal with are often huge. Because of this, they often run into the risk of missing the forests for the trees.

This has led to the single greatest breakthrough in digital marketing technology in recent years: the marriage of Artificial Intelligence with Marketing Automation.

Applications of AI

Artificial Intelligence isn't one specific technology with one specific use in digital marketing. Rather, it's a far-reaching concept that offers virtually limitless possibilities. Marketers often consider AI to be the future of digital marketing, but that's far from the truth. AI isn't the future, it's the present. A number of processes such as audience targeting and ads optimization are already run by AI technology. However, while AI is definitely prevalent today, the applications it finds today are barely the tip of the iceberg when you consider what it is actually capable of.

But before that, let's take a step back and understand what Artificial Intelligence is anyway. For the uninitiated, Artificial Intelligence is, in simple terms, a series of learned processes. AI technology can be seen as a form or machine learning, where repeated actions are understood and then improvised. This function of Artificial Intelligence lends itself perfectly to the next big avenue of digital marketing technology: marketing automation.

With the volume of consumer data, ad variations and platform optimizations available, marketers can often find too much of their time going into tweaking the finer aspects of the larger digital strategy. While this analysis requires a lot of time, it is still extremely important because when it comes to digital marketing, the devil is in the details. With marketing automation, however, most of these processes can be automated to produce faster and more accurate results. Thus, a marketer doesn't have to manually sift through volumes of data to perform an analysis, the machine does it for them.

In the entire digital marketing ecosystem, there are a number of activities that can be automated with ease. Some of them include:

- **Email and SMS marketing:** Rather than sending out bulk emails or SMSes, AI-powered marketing automation can help determine the right mix of emails and SMS-es to send out depending upon the interest levels of a consumer and the actions they have taken in the past. This level of personalization can lead to higher response rates and conversions.

- **Lead management:** Marketing automation in the lead management cycle can improve efficiency of the marketing and sales teams. Leads generated can be designated as sales-ready depending upon set parameters, allowing sales teams greater visibility.

- **Workflow management:** Several parts of a business' workflow can be automated for greater coordination between teams and more efficient processes.

- **Social media automation:** Automation of social media activity can reduce the amount of time you spend on your brand's social media accounts. Automation can help schedule posts, determine the right targeting mix and provide in-depth analysis to power future campaign ideas.

- **Analytics and data visualization:** Analytics is often considered the meat of marketing automation. The huge volume of data available at a digital marketer's fingertips is only as good as their analysis of it. Marketing automation that uses AI technology can recognize patterns in large volumes of data and provide concise inferences within a fraction of the time it would take for a human to perform the same task.

Reaping the Benefits of Marketing Automation

Marketing automation is far from just a snazzy new feature to add to your marketing process; it can be make or break. Possibly the most touted benefit of marketing automation is that it saves time. But AI and marketing automation actually offer benefits that go far beyond that. If you decide to add or upgrade your marketing automation, there are some key benefits that you can expect to witness.

- **More accurate targeting**

  Generating high-quality leads with minimal spillover is the ultimate goal of any business. If your audience targeting is not tightly and accurately defined, you might be leaking your marketing budget on the wrong audience or generating poor-quality leads that have little-to-no likelihood of converting. Marketing automation can help prevent these pitfalls by understanding who the best target audience is based on historical performance. Automation can also identify which stage of the decision making funnel your audience falls into based on their behaviour on your website or your ads. This can help serve up more targeted messaging that has a higher chance of converting.

- **Converting leads to customers through lead nurturing**

  The bottom line for any company is to get higher sales. While generating a high number of leads is a means to achieve this, it's important to remember that not all leads convert into actual customers. To encourage your leads to make the final purchase decision (and re-purchase if they already have), you need to have a hyper-personalized lead nurturing strategy. Marketing automation tools allow you to create custom segments for your leads and then deliver consistent messages based on their specific interests, pain points and needs. This can help your messaging resonate better and convert your leads to loyal customers.

- **Improved ROI on marketing**

    When done right, the full spectrum of capabilities that AI and marketing automation offer will ultimately help you achieve a higher ROI on your marketing activities. This is done in a number of ways. The most obvious way is by optimizing your targeting and ad spends so that you have a higher lead-to-conversion percentage. But in the longer run, automation can also help personalize your customer's experience with your brand, shorten the lead cycle, improve loyalty and return purchases and give you valuable consumer insights which you can leverage to improve both your product offerings and your communication strategy. Which marketer can say no to that!

Human, but Better?

With the growing sophistication of AI and marketing automation, there are understandably concerns from many quarters that the machines might, in fact, overtake humans in most digital marketing operations. After all, for many tasks like analysis and optimization, AI isn't just replacing humans, but is in fact, doing them *better*! So is this a cause for concern? Do digital marketers need to keep an eye out and develop a new hobby in case their day job is lost to R2D2? Fortunately, no.

The reason for this is in the very definition of AI. Right now, AI's greatest strength is also its biggest limitation. Artificial Intelligence understands, replicates and optimizes *learned* processes. If there are certain repetitive tasks or clearly defined parameters, AI immediately outshines humans. But when it comes to work that involves creativity, innovative thinking and intuition, the machines just aren't a match for the little grey cells.

Because of this, AI isn't necessarily a competitor, but an enabler. With automation taking care of most time-consuming repetitive tasks, human marketers have more time freed up to focus on developing strategies that actually add value.

Artificial Intelligence and marketing automation are here to stay. With the adoption of smarter technology and processes, businesses can see a huge improvement in their digital performance and higher profit margins.

Chapter 19

Pushing the Boundaries of Reality: AR and VR

Human beings today are practically bionic; constantly hooked onto an electronic device. But with advances in technology, the lines between the real world and the virtual world are set to become even more blurred.

When Back to the Future 2 first premiered in 1989, it presented to its audience a glitzy, sci-fi view of what the future would be like. Set in the impossibly distant year of 2015, the movie is filled with magical technology like flying cars, hoverboards, massive flat screen TVs, virtual assistants and even self-tying shoelaces. 2015 finally came and reality was very different from the one predicted over two decades ago. Most technology, like flying cars, shown in the movie were still the stuff of fantasy, but one very important invention had come true: 'video glasses'. In the movie, people could wear a set of special glasses and watch a video in a way that made you feel like you were experiencing it in real life.

Virtual Reality and Augmented Reality have burst into the scene and their applications extend far beyond being able to watch videos on a pair of goggles. For a while after its inception though, AR and VR were mostly considered snazzy buzzwords that can make your brand look 'cool' but don't deliver any tangible results. Today, however, they can be one of the most integral parts of your digital marketing strategy. What has acted as a catalyst for this shift? The worldwide COVID-19 pandemic of 2019.

The COVID-19 pandemic and the ensuing lockdown brought the entire world to a standstill. Simple things most of us took for granted like watching a movie in a theatre with a 100 other people or going out to eat in a restaurant were now distant memories. The pandemic caused most of our actual reality to be confined to the four walls of our homes. To expand our horizons, virtual reality suddenly became the answer that was right under our nose. All of a sudden, virtual city tours, museum tours, concerts and sports tournaments were high in demand. Virtual reality became the closest way to regain essential parts of the human experience.

Here are some of the most promising applications of AR and VR in digital marketing strategies of the future.

Bringing Your Product into Your Customer's World

Some of the frontrunners of AR and VR are real estate brands and retail. Both these categories (real estate in particular), have long depended upon customers visiting their store or model apartment, exploring it for themselves and only then choosing to purchase it. But with virtual reality, potential buyers can get a feel of the property as if they were in the actual location, while sitting on their living room sofa. AR also has extensive applications in retail, where customers can try on different glasses frames (something which Lenskart has started offering extensively), try on makeup to see if the shade matches them, even put together an entire ensemble before actually purchasing it. With the lines between virtual and actual reality becoming increasingly blurred, hitherto offline players stand to make huge strides in the online space.

Drive Engagement like Never Before

We have spoken about engagement extensively in almost every chapter of the book because it really is one of the most crucial metrics for a brand. However, the engagement from almost every traditional channel of digital marketing pales in comparison to what AR and VR can deliver. These technologies have the advantage of still being novel and practically *made* for users to interact with. One only has to think about the Pokemon Go craze that gripped the world in 2016 to see the power of AR. Any technology that can get teenagers to leave their homes and walk around their city in the search for mythical creatures is a technology worth reckoning with. Even smaller scale AR offerings like AR filters on Instagram have shown unprecedented levels of engagement. Thus, if you want to capture the imagination of your audience, investing in AR and VR is highly recommended.

Case Study: How we increased engagement and awareness for Tata CLiQ on Instagram during the pandemic

Industry: E-commerce

Objective: To create a heartwarming campaign dedicated to adults working from home during the lockdown to remind, reassure and make their audience rejoin in nostalgia of their good ol' office days.

Strategy: A few brands had already narrated this tale via the stories of employees and the things they miss about office, but none of them had done it from the perspective of the stories of office and things that it misses about people. Thus #YouMadeItCliq was born. A campaign of the office, by the office but for the employees.

Since Tata CLiQ wanted to improve their Instagram engagement and fortunately since our target audience were also spending time indoors, online, there was never a better opportunity to use AR Filters on Instagram.

We came up with an interesting AR filter that helps the users to tag an office friend they miss the most. This process created a chain of UGC content. In order to improve the reach of this filter and therefore the campaign, we teamed up with 25+ influencers on Instagram.

On social media, users would believe in the messaging and services of the brand if it comes from anyone but the brand. This user behavior gave us the opportunity to use social discovery channels and platforms which had far more reach than Tata CLiQ on Instagram to showcase our video. This process not only multiplied our reach capabilities but also improved the authenticity of our message.

We also created a series of doodles and comic-based static assets on Instagram to help increase our campaigns reach.

Business Impact:

The video along with the static posts was promoted on Instagram to a pan-India working-class audience and garnered more engagement and reach using Facebook's RnF buying technique.

- 3.9 million+ people reached through the campaign
- 6.4 million+ impressions
- 2.7 lakh+ engagements
- 3.5 lakh+ video views
- 4.9k+ filter captures

Bring Your Tribe Closer

The bedrock for the success of any brand is the tribe you create around the philosophies of your brand. This tribe becomes advocates for your brand, remains loyal despite competition and adopts the brand ethos as a part of their own personal identity. One of the most crucial ways to keep your tribe strong is to bring them together and foster the sense of community. While interacting with them on social media is one way to do it, VR could actually be one of the most effective ways to bring people together. The COVID-19 pandemic has forced concerts, sporting events, even fashion shows, to be held virtually. This has expanded what everyone thought possible with VR. Now, as people continue to be wary of being in crowded spaces, the use of VR events is likely to only grow from here. Brands can use this opportunity to host events for their followers and strengthen their community, while simultaneously increasing their reach and welcoming new members into the fold. Many fitness brands have used this strategy incredibly effectively, organizing group workouts online at a time when public gyms and studios are shut.

Spin a Compelling Story

Tyrion Lannister wasn't wrong when he said that stories maketh a king. Your audience loves being told a powerful story, but they like it better when they're in control of how it goes. Every campaign you create is in it's own way spinning your brand story. VR campaigns work in much the same way, only the experience they offer your audience is incomparably more immersive. When you have captured the senses and imagination of your audience, you have a chance to create a powerful memory in them that can translate into greater affinity towards your brand. VR also lets your users dictate how the story unfolds. They can help the protagonist make a choice and change the course of events. This gets your audience even more engaged with the story.

Recreate an 'Impulse Buy' Retail Setting

If you think back to the last few times you visited a grocery store or a mall, chances are you might remember picking up something you probably didn't plan on buying and purchasing it on an impulse. For retail brands, this split second decision to purchase a product on a whim is crucial. Because of this, entire store layouts are planned in such a way to give you ample opportunity to make an impulse purchase. Sweets are stacked by the checkout counter and new arrivals are invitingly laid out in an aspirational setting. On digital channels, it's more difficult to recreate this scenario, as users have a lot more options to peruse through, are in charge of what kind of products they see and have more access to research before they decide to purchase a product.

Virtual reality, however, can help you recreate in-store shopping experiences. TATA CliQ, for example, launched a virtual mall, replete with storefront displays and branded outlets. Users could 'visit' stores, explore products and even purchase them. The engagement of VR coupled with the ease of buying of e-commerce makes for a powerful combination that can deliver incredible results.

Augmented Reality and Virtual Reality are two of the most exciting avenues of digital marketing because we still haven't even scraped the surface of what these technologies are capable of. The playing field is still open and brands have every opportunity to push the envelope and offer an experience like no other to their audience.

Chapter 20

The Growth of Voice Commerce

"Speak and it shall be done!" Online shopping and navigation was already easy, but voice technology has improved it even further. With the potential to make the internet more accessible to all sections of users, voice technology is one of the most exciting new frontiers in digital marketing.

Online retail has always been about removing hurdles standing in between you, your shopping cart and the checkout counter. Same-day delivery and next-day delivery reduced the time a consumer had to wait for before receiving their product. Doorstep deliveries (especially for groceries) reduced the hassles of having to lug around heavy shopping bags. Subscription services ensured that you didn't have to go a single day without your essential products. The gamut of payment options offered ensured that you can always conveniently checkout, whether you have your card on hand, prefer UPI wallets or old-school cash on delivery. An emerging technology promises to simplify the online buying experience even further.

Imagine you're at home, lounging on a lazy Sunday, when all of a sudden, you realize you're out of your favourite shampoo. Rather than picking up your phone, you simply turn towards your trusty voice assistant and deliver the command, "Alexa, order my shampoo". The next day, a package arrives at your doorstep; sure enough, it's the exact brand of shampoo you requested for.

Voice commerce takes ease of purchase to the next level. It doesn't matter whether you're driving, in the shower or in the middle of cooking yourself dinner; one quick command is all it takes to purchase a product. In India, this technology has special significance. Many of India's new smartphone users (a segment we will be taking a closer look at in the next chapter) have newfound access to the world, but might not know the language to be able to navigate through it. With voice commerce, literacy is no longer a hurdle. As long as the website or app is able to detect the language, a user has virtually no limitations to what they can do on the internet.

Voice Assistants are Getting Smarter

While voice commerce certainly has the potential to be the future of e-commerce, its applications in the present are still limited. If a customer chooses to make a purchase through a voice command, it is most likely to be a repeat order (like in the shampoo example). The percentage of users who use voice to explore and find new products is miniscule. There are a number of possible reasons for this. Consumers are generally careful before placing an order for a new product. They want to find out the supposed benefits of the product, compare it with similar products, view it from all angles and read the reviews before choosing to buy it. Voice searches, obviously, cannot cater to the entire spectrum of the journey. Because of this, consumers tend to revert to their trusty smartphones when they are in the product discovery phase.

But with advancements in voice assistant technology, Alexa might soon know you better than you know yourself. Voice assistants can collate data of your past purchases and use their algorithm to find products that best match your preferences and buying behaviour. Rather than you having to scroll through endless lists of products before shortlisting the ones you're most interested in, your voice assistant can recommend one for you. While this technology has already been rolled out, the accuracy of results is likely to get even more fine-tuned in the near future.

E-Commerce Brands need to get Chattier

E-commerce brands tend to rely on a long reel of pictures to give consumers an idea of what to expect from the actual product. But with voice commerce, these images are redundant because a voice user will not have a chance to glance through them. Instead, another feature of the product has gained renewed importance: the product description. The need for optimized product descriptions from an SEO standpoint were always understood. But now, apart from adding the right keywords, brands need to also ensure that their descriptions paint a vivid image of the product, its uses and its benefits to the user. When a voice assistant reads out the product description, users should feel like they have enough information to not require a second level of research.

Along with product descriptions, voice assistants also read out product reviews. If your product does not have reviews, you stand a chance to lose the customer mid-journey. More interested customers might resort to their phones to check reviews online before making a purchase, but many will simply lose interest and move to a competitor product. To keep your customer with you throughout their buying journey, you need to ensure that all the information they require is discoverable through voice queries. If you haven't already, this is the time to enable reviews and encourage past customers to leave reviews after making a purchase.

Adapting SEO for Voice Commerce

SEO has come a long way since its early days of keyword stuffing, but incorporating the right mix of keywords in your content still remains the bedrock of organic discoverability. With the advent of voice commerce, e-commerce optimization is likely to undergo a massive transformation. To understand the reason for this, all you need to do is think about how you would search for a pair of formal shoes on textual search and on voice search. If you were typing it out, you would probably search for something like, "coconut oil conditioner". Conventional SEO keyword research is used to this and will throw up multiple results that are optimized for this keyword. But if you were to search for it through voice, you would probably say, "Can you show me conditioner brands which have coconut in them?". In this scenario, traditional keyword optimization goes out the window.

When optimizing your product descriptions or website pages for voice search, it's important to remember that the interaction is always going to be conversational. To cater to this new style of navigation, you can make your website or product content into question and answer style. In this way, your content can anticipate questions that potential customers are likely to have and provide accurate answers to them. This will not only help your content match search queries, but can also drive conversions through voice searches.

Voice commerce is making waves all across the globe, but its growth in India is taking a remarkably different trajectory. It isn't just elite users with access to voice assistants like Alexa and Google Home that are driving the segment, but vernacular users who are faced with a novel territory for the first time. This has led to numerous home-grown voice-based companies that offer vernacular voice search services, which can help audiences from non-metro cities navigate the world wide web with ease. In the next chapter, we will be learning more about this next generation of internet users and see how they are shaping India's online behaviour.

CHAPTER 21

The Explosion of Vernacular Content

English has long been the lingua franca of the world wide web, but not for long. Increasing access to smartphones has made India's digital space a lot more diverse and exciting. Digital strategies, therefore, cannot depend solely on the existing internet users, but on the next wave of vernacular users.

The average Indian internet user a few years ago looked very different from what an average Indian internet user looks like today. In the not-so-distant past, an Indian who had regular access to the internet usually lived in an urban city, communicated online largely through English (the lingua franca of the virtual world) and seamlessly switched between browsing the internet on their computer and through their phone. Today, the Indian internet landscape looks completely different. It's democratic, it's diverse and it spans across socio-economic stratas. But the internet was by no means new in India. Over the last 10 years, India has developed a reputation as one of the world's leading IT service providers. What then acted as a sudden catalyst to the explosion of the internet within a relatively short period of time?

From Cybercafes to Cell Phones

Until a few years ago, one of the biggest status symbols a conspicuous spender could have was not necessarily the swankiest mansion or the most expensive car; it was something much smaller and yet more powerful: a smartphone. A smartphone showed the world that you could connect to the internet from wherever you were, that you could afford to pay the high price tag most smartphones came with and you could easily pay the high monthly phone bills that internet usage invariably led to. For the rest of the masses, accessing the world through the palm of their hand was unthinkable. If a person had to access the internet, they might have a desktop at home if they were lucky, or more commonly, they would have to pay by the minute at the local cyber cafe. The deeper you got into the interior of India, the more far apart these centres would be – if they even existed.

But the potential of India's massive unconnected audience did not go unnoticed. One has to only look back as recently as Facebook's controversial Free Basics plan to see that getting India's population online has long been a priority for the gatekeepers of the internet. However, the best way to do so remained unclear. Until two critical factors changed the Indian internet landscape forever.

The first big change was the introduction of low-cost smartphones. Low-cost phones had existed for some time in the market, but apart from making calls and sending SMS-es, the owner could do little else with them. Low-cost smartphones, on the other hand, finally provided a way for millions of Indians to navigate through the world wide web. These affordable smartphones provided many of the same features as higher-end ones at only a fraction of the cost. Because of this, India's journey to coming online followed a very different path from most developed countries. The conventional model was to progress from desktops with dial-up connections, to laptops and then to mobile phones. But for most Indians, the high price tag of desktops and laptops put them completely out of their reach. Instead, a huge majority of India skipped the PC stage entirely and went directly to the smartphone stage. The implications of this are many. For one, having a mobile-first approach is all the more important in India because most consumers will never even have a chance to navigate your online presence through anything other than a smartphone.

The second big change was the introduction of low-cost mobile data. Mobile data has customarily been expensive in India and could have easily impeded the online revolution in the country. After all, what use was an affordable smartphone if the internet was too expensive to access anyway?

Luckily, the burst of low-cost smartphones on the scene coincided with the arrival of incredibly affordable high-speed internet. In early September 2016, Reliance Jio announced the launch of its new telecom and mobile broadband services at rates that were a fraction of the contemporary market prices. One month from that announcement, Jio had 16 million subscribers and by February of 2017, the number had crossed 100 million. This was the fastest increase any telecom provider had ever seen. The effect on the market was immediate. Rival telecom brands were forced to push down their rates to compete on the market and all of a sudden, mobile data wasn't an unaffordable luxury anymore.

These two coinciding factors led to the birth of a new chapter in India's internet story.

What does the Internet Landscape Look like Today?

The democratization of the internet in India meant that internet access wasn't just open to the urban English-speaking elite, but to all sections of society. Suddenly, there was an explosion of languages and cultural backgrounds on the internet, making the virtual world as diverse as the country itself.

Hindi, unsurprisingly has the widest reach among new internet users, however, other regional languages appear to have the highest adoption levels. Tamil has the highest adoption rate, with 33 percent in 2016 and a projected 53% by 2021. Other South Indian languages like Kannada and Telugu also dominate the online sphere.

(source: KPMG – Indian Languages Defining India's Internet)

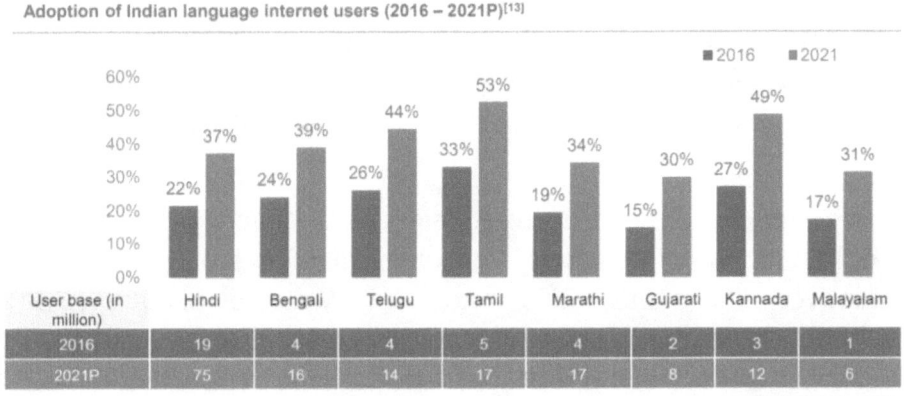

The newfound accessibility to the internet dramatically altered the online space as well the new users. Indian internet users from tier 2 and 3 cities and beyond were suddenly exposed to the seductive world of internet consumerism in a big way. Influencer culture, the constant bombardment of ads and online streaming platforms created new dreams and aspirations among them. In turn, the online world has to adapt quickly to the changing audience base. Non-metro audiences have been increasingly shown to prefer ads served in their local language, lighter websites that can load faster on 2G mobile connections and mobile-first interfaces which can be easily navigated through their smartphones.

The extent to which brands were able to fulfill these demands in their digital strategy determined whether they retained or repelled a non-metro consumer. The pay-offs of capturing a vernacular user are massive and is increasingly becoming a make-or-break factor for brands.

Case Study: How we devised a robust strategy for Khatabook to rank #1 on Google Play Store by driving over 10 million app installs

Industry: Consumer apps

Objective: To increase the volume of installs followed by retention of those users by logging in as the 1st touchpoint and further, adding in new customers by leveraging vernacular content

Strategy: For the first campaign, we leveraged multiple combinations of creative resources like video ads, HTML creatives, static ads, GIFs, text ads. We also used the ad scheduling feature as we wanted to sustain the budgets over a longer period of time to yield better results. While the first campaigns were focused on installs, we soon moved to run campaigns optimized for in-app events.

Innovation in tapping into newer markets

Our competitors focused only on Hindi as a language of communication. We saw the need for a vernacular approach and helped devise a strategy to reach out to the untapped Southern Market. We started with top-languages like Telugu followed by Tamil.

Revamping Google Search Strategy

Google search strategy was revamped to increase visibility to the high intent audiences, and stay on top-of-the-mind to those relevant.

As UACe campaigns were still not approved, we ran basic retargeting and remarketing ads. We built custom affinity audiences with competitor Apps and reached out to them by targeting them on Display. In our communication, we highlighted key USPs as to why KhataBook is better than competitors.

> **Tapping into TikTok for new audience**
>
> We played with bids and content to increase relevance and optimization based on results. This helped establish Tik Tok as one of the important pillars for customer acquisition.
>
> We spoke to inactive users who had previously frequently used the App and then stopped to understand the reason for drop-off and implemented their queries in the newer versions of the App. This helped increase daily and monthly active users. We also started UACe campaigns on Google to help increase re-engagement with the App users and drive key steps within the App.
>
> **Business Impact:**
>
> - Ranked #1 on Google Playstore
> - 10 million+ app installs

The (Vernacular) Customer is King

A strong vernacular strategy has evolved from a 'nice-to-have' feature in a brand's overall digital marketing strategy, to one of the most critical factors for its strategy to succeed. This is because non-metro audiences aren't just spending more time online, but they're also more willing to spend their money. Many areas have seen a rise in their disposable income and that coupled with higher aspirations makes these consumers a critical market for brands.

What's interesting is that the demand in non-metro cities isn't just for affordable low-to-mid category goods, but for products and services across price categories. In fact, one report by CII-MRB predicted that tier 2 and 3 cities will be the main drivers of the luxury goods market. The same report found that the primary motivation behind spending on big-ticket items is largely the same, whether a consumer is a resident of a metro or a tier 3 town. Most men surveyed wanted to purchase products that would signify their status, while women wanted to indulge themselves in the latest fashions.

Largely, however, non-metro online spending is largely directed towards the purchase of electronic goods. One of the possible reasons for this could be a complete game changer for brands. A 2016 study by Google and KPMG posited that the reason why electronics sales perform so well in non-metro markets is because most of these brands and platforms have adapted quickly and serve up content in a number of regional languages. Other product categories like fashion, beauty and lifestyle lag behind because of a lack of regional language communication.

This shows that non-metro markets are one of the largest untapped resources at a brand's disposal. The start of the decade has witnessed an expansion of social media platforms that are largely targeted towards regional users and an increasing awareness of the power that non-metro consumers hold.

Appendix: Digital Marketing Jargon Busters

Social Media Marketing

1. API (Application Programming Interface): This is a software that allows two applications to interact with each other. It sends the request from the customer to the provider and delivers the provider's response back to the customer. It runs and delivers data from a website or application to the customer when customer's request for the data, thus creating a system of connectivity.

2. Engagement Rate: This shows how many people or the audience are interacting with the content that is put online. The Engagement Rate measures the level of engagement that a piece of content creates. Shares, likes, re-tweets are factors that influence the Engagement.

3. Impressions: This refers to the number of times that your content was displayed or how often your ad is shown. An impression is counted each time your ad is shown regardless of whether it has been clicked on or not.

4. **Social Media Influencer:** These are people who use social media platforms such as Instagram, Facebook etc. to establish a sense of credibility for themselves to promote what they do in a specific industry. These people have a large following and can persuade others due to their reach.

5. **Geo Tagging:** This refers to when a geographical location is added to any kind of meta data online, such as photos, video, messages, QR codes, websites etc.

6. **Conversion Rate:** Conversion rate refers to the number of sales or conversions divided by the total number of visitors. For example if a website has about 150 visitors in a month and they make about 50 sales, then the conversion rate will be 25/150 = 33%.

7. **Firehose data:** We need a way to stream data as it continues to update to users on the internet like a firehose. A firehose API is a steady stream of all the available data from a particular source that gets updated in real time, and this delivers data to any number of subscribers in real time.

8. **Historical Data:** These refer to data that exists in the past, and is used as a basic so that future trends and data can be predicted.

9. **Natural Language Processing (NLP):** This is a field which is mostly concerned with interactions between computers and human languages, and how computers can analyze and program natural or human languages.

10. **Machine Learning:** These are a set of computer algorithms that will update and improve automatically from experience. It is related to the concept of Artificial intelligence where machines and technology learn with time and experience.

11. **Reach:** Reach refers to the total number of people who are exposed to the ad through a medium, at least once, during a given period. This is not equal to the number of people who will potentially be exposed to ads in the future.

Appendix: Digital Marketing Jargon Busters | **173**

12. Social Retargeting: This is also called Social remarketing. This is an online method of advertising of reaching out to the previous visitors or users of your website or application. This can help in capturing leads if customers left your site without meeting the marketing goal.

13. Social ROI: Social Return on Investment is a method that organizations use to account for the creation of value. It helps to enable how much change is really being created by tracking social, economic and environmental results.

14. Total Potential Impressions: This refers to the total number of potential audience who will see your content. For example, on Instagram or Twitter, you Total Potential Impressions are your total number of followers.

15. Viral: This is phenomena which occurs when any image, piece of information like an article or blog, or a video is circulated widely and quickly on the internet.

16. Visualizations: Media visualization refers to the analysis of images and visual media and uses processing techniques to make visual spaces of the information that has been analyzed.

17. Social Media Audit: This is a process of making a review of what is working, what is not, what is failing and what can be done to improve the content across all of your social media.

18. Social Media Analytics: This is the process of gathering data from across the social media channels and then analyzing them using analysing tools to make decisions for business.

19. A/B Testing: This is a user experience research method. The sample is divided into two groups A and B and the market idea is tested on both the groups separately to see how they would react. This helps to avoid risks and determine conversions and loyalty of the customers.

20. Ads Manager: This is the starting point for displaying and running your ads on Facebook, Instagram etc. You can create, manage as well as track your ads with this tool.

21. Audience Profiling: This refers to figuring out who your actual target audience is by observing the consumer's buying behaviour across many platforms.

22. Boost post: This is a type of paid advertisement on Facebook which promotes an already existing post on a business page. These amplify the content reach so that the post appears on more people's pages who do not follow you.

23. Brand advocacy: This refers to making your brand seem good in the eyes of the consumer through word of mouth marketing. Brand advocates give positive reviews about the brand products and this forms a large part in the strategy of marketing as many consumers depend on reviews and social recommendations before buying a product.

24. ORM: Online reputation management is monitoring, addressing or removing certain Search Engine Result Pages or certain web or online media mentions. Mentions on social media can be a benefit if it is a positive statement but can be a threat if the brand is criticised.

25. Relevance Score: This is calculated based on the negative and positive feedback that the brand expects to receive from its target audience. The higher the expected positive feedback the higher the relevance score.

26. Sentiment analysis: This refers to an analysis of what the customer feels about the brand or it's products such as opinions, emotions, attitudes, appraisals etc. It is the process of categorizing opinions as positive, negative or neutral.

27. Social listening: This is the process of monitoring your brand's social media channels for any customer feedback or direct mentions regarding certain keywords or opportunities or competitors.

28. Carousel ads: These ads combine many pictures or videos in a single ad thus making the ad visually appealing, interesting and engaging.

Content Marketing

1. Blogging: This refers to the process of making blogs. Blogs are somewhat like online journals, where people create their stories, opinions or other information in the form of writing, pictures and videos to share with other people and users online.

2. Analytics: Google Analytics is a site that reports as well as tracks traffic on your website and it is a site that is of great help to marketers.. It studies past data to reveal potential for new trends.

3. Call to action: This is a marketing term such as the use of words or phrases, which are used to prompt a response from the consumer or push the consumer to make a sale immediately.

4. Evergreen Content: This is the kind of content that never really goes out data. It does not matter what the cycle of news is or what the season is. It is always relevant to the readers.

5. Keywords: These are terms that are relevant to the information that a user is searching for. Website owners generally Find and research alternative items related to their website that users might look up so that their site comes up first in the results page.

6. Social Optimization: SMO or Social Media Optimization is the process of increasing awareness about a product or a brand by using many social media outlets and channels to generate publicity.

7. Visual Content: This is content on any kind of online platform that is based on images. These can include pictures, videos, diagrams, infographics, animated GIFS, memes etc.

8. Pillar Content: This is content that provides the complete answer to any question that the user is asking or searching about a given topic. This is made to provide the reader with

value and so that the website can rank highly on the search engines

9. **Dynamic Content:** This is content on the internet that changes based on the interest, preferences and behaviour of the user – such as social networking sites which provide different kinds of content based on the user.

10. **Buyer Persona:** This is a representation of who your target audience actually is based on data that has been collected and market research about the existing consumers. This generally includes customer demographics, goals and motivations.

11. **UGC:** This is also called User Generated Content. This is content that is created by other users – instead of the brand promoting itself, user's promote the brands products by posting content that features the brands product and services..

12. **Data-backed Content:** This kind of content includes data as data is one of the main indicators of content that is trustworthy, and if the content is trustworthy, it ends up being persuasive.

13. **Experimental Content:** This refers to content that is created in a manner that is not usually a manner that the company would follow or do. It departs from what is normal or what is expected of the company.

14. **Inbound Link:** This is also known as a backlink. An inbound link for a particular page is a link present on some other website that leads back to that page. These links point to your websites from other websites.

15. **Infographic:** These are graphic representations of information or data that are made to present information clearly and very quickly so that it is easy to read.

16. **CMS:** This is known as a Content Management System. This is a software that manages the creation as well as the modification of content created for the internet.

17. Drip Email: This term is used when emails that include a pre-written set of messages are sent to customers as well as prospective customers over a period of time ultimately leading to a call to action.

18. Email Workflows: These are a bunch of automated emails that are sent out based on the customer data or behaviour. This is generally done for generating new leads. This email are assembled to accomplish a goal such as following new leads or onboarding new customers.

19. Bounce Rate: This refers to the number of people who visit a site on the internet and then leave after viewing just one page of the site and not the other pages. This is used during web traffic analysis.

20. Organic traffic: This refers to viewers who land on your page due to unpaid or organic search results. They do not arrive as a result of paid promotions done by the company.

21. Referral traffic: This refers to how many people viewed your website outside of the search engine results. Some people may visit your site through hyperlinks – this counts as a referral visit.

22. Guest posts: This refers to writing and publishing an article on someone else's blog or website and you get a link to your website or blog in return.

23. InMail: This is a LinkedIn service that lets you send messages to other LinkedIn users even if you are not connected to them. It is available to those who have a premium LinkedIn account.

24. Display ad network: Display ad networks take ads from your company and they show them on websites according to your specifications and it attracts customers from other sites that your company normally would not be able to reach.

SEO

1. **Branded Keywords:** These are keywords that include your website or brand name or variations of it. These are basically keywords that are unique to your brand or domain.

2. **Click through Rate:** This is the ratio of the number of users who click on a particular link to the total number of users who view the email, page, ad or website.

3. **Conversion Rate Optimization (CRO):** This refers to the process of raising the percentage of people who visit a website and push them to take the desired action or become customers.

4. **Cost per Acquisition (CPA):** This refers to the cost of acquiring one paying consumer through a channel or campaign. It is calculated by dividing the total cost by the number of customers obtained through that particular channel.

5. **Cost Per Click (CPC):** This is a term which is used when the advertisers pays a certain commission for the publisher of the ad when the ad is clicked on by a user or viewer.

6. **Cross Linking:** This refers to the linking of one site with another, thereby allowing the user to reference sites that are similar to what they are already viewing and sites that may be of further interest to them.

7. **Google Ads:** This is an online advertising platform by Google where advertisers pay google to display their products, video ads, service offerings, brief advertisements etc. within the google ad

8. **Backlink:** This is also known as an inbound link. An inbound link for a particular page is a link present on some other website that leads back to that page. These links point to your websites from other websites.

9. **Anchor Text:** This refers to the text that is clickable in a hyperlink or an HTML text. This is generally shown as a blue coloured text which is underlined.

10. **Broken Link:** A broken link is when the link on a web page no longer works because the website may be encountering certain errors such as the website may have removed the linked web page.

11. **Canonical URL (Canonical Tag):** This is a way of telling search engines that a specific URL represents the main copy of a page. This prevents problems that can be caused by duplicate or identical content.

12. **Click Bait:** This is a form of advertisement that uses text or thumbnail that is designed in such a way to attract or entice the users so that they click on the link to follow, view or read the content.

13. **Content Management System:** These are a set of functions, processes and technologies that support the management, collection and the publishing of information in any kind of forum or medium.

14. **Content Syndication:** This refers to when any content on the web is reposted or re-published by a third party. This content could refer to blogs, videos, articles, pictures etc. This is sort of like a barter arrangement where the third party gets free content and the original publisher of the content get's publicity.

15. **Cornerstone Content:** This refers to the best and the most important pieces of content that you want to show on your site and the posts or pages that you want to rank highly in the search engines.

16. **Content curation:** This refers to the process of gathering content that is relevant to a particular area or topic of interest with the intention of adding value to a piece of content.

17. **De-indexing:** This refers to when for some reason, a particular webpage or web site or any kind of web-based content, is taken out of that index and therefore does not show up in the search engine results.

18. Domain authority: This describes the relevance of a particular website or webpage in a specific area of industry. This has a direct impact on it's search engine ranking.

19. Google Algorithm: This is a system which retrieves data from the search index and then tries to show the best results for any query that has been asked by a user.

20. Black hat SEO: These refer to strategies and tactics to get higher search engine rankings and breaking the rules. This concerns itself mostly with search engines and not the impact on the human audience. Examples can include Keyword stuffing, or Reporting a competitor.

21. White hat SEO: This is the opposite of Black Hat SEO. It refers to the practice of improving your search rankings on the search engine results page by staying within the terms of service of search engines.

22. Crawling: This refers to when google or any other search engine sends bots to your website to read and analyze the content on it. This is the first step that is done before your site is recognized by the search engine in the results page.

23. Do follow links: These are HTML links that allow search bots to follow the link on that website. It sort of passes the authority from the website that is referred to the Linked website. This increases the page rank in the search engine results.

24. E.A.T.: Google E.A.T is a popular acronym that stands for the main 3 requirements that google considers while determining the quality of content on a page – Expertise, Authority and Trustworthiness.

25. Email Outreach: This refers to contacting people via email. This can be used to generate leads, create a network, promote services or even get influencers.

26. Featured Snippet: This is a summary of the answer to the user's query and this is displayed on top of the search engine

results. It includes the content from the page, the title and URL.

27. Keyword cannibalization: This happens when you have multiple pages on the same site which target the same keyword. When there is more than one page for a single keyword, your pages end up competing with themselves.

28. Link Building: This describes the ways that are aimed at increasing the quality and the number of inbound links in a web page with the main goal of increasing the rankings on the search engines results page.

29. Meta title: This is the head section of an HTML link, that shows the title of each website to tell the users what the website entails. It is used by search engines to show the results on the results page.

30. Meta description: This is a snippet of about 155 characters which summarizes the content of a particular page. Search engines show it in the results page when the term that is searched for appears in the description.

31. No-follow link: These are links with the No-follow tag applied to them, which basically tell search engines to ignore that as they do not impact the search engine rankings of a page.

32. ON-page SEO: This refers to optimizing web pages so that they rank higher in the search engine results page, by optimizing the content and the HTML source code – basically anything on the website.

33. Off-page SEO: This refers to the actions of optimization that are taken outside of the website to increase the rankings of the page on the search engine results such as external links.

34. Rich snippet: In a rich snippet there is extra information that is given between the URL and the main description. There might also be a picture included, so that search engines can better understand what the website content is about.

35. Schema: This refers to a vocabulary of tags that you can add to your content to improve the way that your page is read and represented by the search engines. Schema.org basically promotes schemas for structured data online.

36. Thin Content: This can be defined as content with very less or no added value. These include pages with duplicate content, scraped content etc.

Digital Advertising

1. Key Performance Indicators (KPI): These are factors on the basis of which the success of an organization or the organizational activities is measured and it is a kind of measurement of performance.

2. Cost per thousand impressions (CPM): This is also known as Cost Per Mille. It is measurement in advertising and it is the cost that an advertiser has to bear for a 1000 views or clicks of an advertisement.

3. Pay per click (PPC): This is an online website traffic driving method where the advertiser pays the publisher of the ad every time a user clicks on the ad.

4. View Through Conversion (VTC): This is a type of conversation tracking in Google which shows how many people saw your display ad on google but did not click on it.

5. Cost per Acquisition (CPA): This is an ad measurement and pricing model that measures the cost to get a paying customer or a channel or on a campaign level.

6. Above The Fold: This is the part of the webpage that is visible in the browser window when the page loads, because users tend to engage more with content above the fold than below the fold.

7. Affiliate Marketing: This is a type of marketing which is performance based, where businesses reward affiliates for

each visitor or customer that is gathered by the affiliate through his or her marketing skills.

8. Contextual Targeting: This is a form of advertising where automated systems select and serve ads on websites and other media based on the context of what the user is looking for.

9. Cost per lead (CPL): This is an advertising model where the advertiser pays for a sign up by the customer who is interested in what the advertiser is offering.

10. Cross-device Targeting: This is a strategy that enables marketers and advertisers to reach out to several users at many touch points such as computers, smartphones, smart TVs.

11. Demand-Side Platform: This is a system that allows digital advertising inventory buyers to manage ad exchanges and data exchange accounts through a single interface.

12. Display Advertising: These refer to graphic advertising on websites, social media, applications, through banners, texts, images, audio or video which are made to deliver ads and brand messages.

13. Interstitial Ads: These are full screen ads that cover almost the entire interface of that app; these are present at transition points in the app like between activities or when the game is paused.

14. Native Advertising: This is a type of advertising that matches the function as well as the form of the platform on which the advertisement appears. These are found on various social media channels and in the form of suggested content.

15. Pop-Up: These are mostly graphic ads that suddenly appear into the foreground of the visual interface that you are using such as a website or an application. They have a 2% click through rate.

16. Programmatic Media Buying: This refers to the sale and purchase of ad space in real time. The software is used

to automate the placement as well as the purchase and optimisation of inventory through a system of bidding.

17. SEM: This stands for search engine marketing and it includes the promotion of websites through increasing the visibility of the websites in the search engine results page.

18. RLSA: Remarketing Lists for Search Ads lets you customize some of your search ad campaigns for those who have visited your site previously and tailor these ads to those visitors when they are searching on google.

19. Frequency capping: This is the limit to the number of times a specific visitor of a certain website is shown the ad. This restriction is applied to almost all websites which contain ads from the same ad network.

20. In-stream video ads: These are ads that are played before, during or after the specific video content that a user is streaming. These are popular on Youtube and Facebook.

21. Bumper ads: These are ads on YouTube that are six seconds, and are unskippable ads that generally play before the YouTube video. These are generally created to extend the reach of a particular campaign.

22. Lookalike audience: This is a popularly used term for Facebook ads, which is a new way to reach a set of people who probably have similar qualities to your existing customer and will be easy to target.

23. Display ad network: These networks connect advertisers to websites that want to host these advertisements. The main function of these networks is to connect the ad supply of the publishers and match them with the demand of the advertiser.

Design

1. Golden Ratio: The Golden Ratio is a shape with a proportion of 1:1.618. This composition is important in design because it not only helps to convey useful information in a simple

manner, but also helps create an aesthetically pleasing layout.

2. Rule of Thirds: This is a rule in design where an image is divided into thirds, horizontally and vertically and the object is placed at the intersection of the lines or along the lines. This is a useful rule when it comes to design as it makes it easier for the eye to read information on images that follow this rule.

3. Kerning: This is the process of adjusting the space between two letters or characters of a certain font so as to make the final result more visually pleasing.

4. Leading: This refers to line spacing or line height and it describes the distance between each line of the given text.

5. Tracking: This refers to tightening or loosening a block of text and refers to the overall spacing of the text.

6. Logotype: This is the part of the logo which refers to the text or an abbreviation or the name of the business which is written in a certain recognizable font that is customized for the company.

7. Logomark: This is the part of the logo which acts like a mark or a symbol that does not contain the name of a business and it is like an image that represents the company.

8. Icon: This is a graphic element that represents something abstract or real and it could represent an action, motive or entity.

9. Style Guide: This refers to a set of standard templates for typing, formatting and presenting a set of documents. There are many templates so you can choose what suits your brand best.

10. Aspect Ratio: This is a design term which is widely used and the aspect ratio of a shape refers to the ratio of the size to the dimensions or in simple terms the ratio of a shape's width and height.

11. Abstract Mark: These refer to vert big ideas being conveyed in a sort of abstract way – these are very conceptual and

they mostly represent values or certain ideas rather than conveying a message.

12. Emblem: This refers to a symbol or a pictorial image that is designed to explain a concept or some sort of moral truth, an allegory or a person.

13. Lettermark: This is a design element that is typography based and is composed of few letters that include the company's initials alone.

14. Pictorial Mark: These often take the shape of iconic logos and can be simple drawings or detailed illustrations. They generally make a quick connection with the audience such as the Twitter logo or the McDonald's logo.

15. Mascot: These are people or animals or objects which are used to represent certain group such as a school, or a team or even a brand name.

16. Wordmark: This refers to a type of logo that includes only the company name and it is a text only logo. They are also known as LogoTypes.

17. Grid: A Grid is used for organizing the layout for print as well as digital purposes such as a website. They are a series of intersecting lines and can be used to plan how the information would go on a page.

18. Web Page Elements: Web Page elements include those things that go on a website such as paragraphs, links, headings, images etc.

19. Breadcrumb Trail: This is sort of a navigation scheme that shows the location of a user in a website or any particular web application. This allows users to keep track and be aware of their location on various programs and sites.

20. Banner: This is a form of advertisement by an ad server which spreads across the webpage and it is intended to increase traffic to a website by linking the site to the advertiser.

21. Wireframe: This is also known as a screen blueprint or the framework of a site and it is a sort of visual guide that shows us how the elements of the Webpage will be placed.

22. Sidebar: These guide the users to related pages such as another product or service, related topics on the website or even other links that the visitor might be interested in.

23. Footer: This section is located under the main section of the page and is probably the last thing a user sees. It has additional information such as contact details and addresses.

24. Navigation Bar: This website element is part of the graphical user interface so as to make it easier for the user to access information on the website and this is an important part of the design element.

25. Header: Generally the above the fold region of the home page is considered the header of the website and is generally the top section of the WebPage. This contains the company logo, a brief history about the company, navigation bar etc.

User Experience

1. Automation Testing: This is a software test technique which compares the actual outcome with the expected one. This is used to automate certain repetitive tasks which are difficult to do manually.

2. Back End Development: Backend development languages handle the 'behind-the-scenes' of applications. This code connects the database to the web, manages connections with the users, and powers the web application.

3. Avatar: This refers to any graphical representation of the user's character. This can be 2D such as an icon on many internet forums or 3D such as characters on many virtual games.

4. Emoticons: These are pictorial representations of facial expressions or characters that people use to express their emotions virtually.

5. Cache: This is the software or the hardware component that stores the data, so that future requests for the same data can be served faster.

6. Customer Relationship Management Software (CRM Software): This software manages the company's interaction with its current customers as well as the potential customers. It helps in customer interaction, generating leads and streamlining this process.

7. Front End Development: The structure, design, interface and behaviour of a mobile application, website, web applications is all implemented by the front end developers.

8. Javascript: This is often abbreviated as JS and is a common programming language used in web development, and it is meant to add interactive and dynamic content on the website.

9. Design Debt: This refers to all the good design ideas that had to be scrapped in order for the company to reach its short term goals, and the company may settle for something simple.

10. End User: In the development of the product, the end user is the person who ultimately uses the product or is intended to use the product.

11. Gamification: This refers to the application of gaming elements into non-gaming contexts. Marketers use gamification to increase consumer engagement and to influence the behaviour of consumers.

12. Heat Map: This is basically a visual snap of all the webpages that highlight the parts of your website that are visited the most and it is a map that shows the user behaviour on your site.

13. Interaction Design: This form of design includes Design strategies, identifying the key interactions of products of the brand, creating many prototypes to test concepts etc.

14. Average Response Time: This refers to the time that an application server takes to get responses to the user when he or she asks a query.

Website Development

1. Responsive Web Design: This is a kind of approach that suggests that the development of a website should be based on the consumer's behaviour and environment and this is based on screen size, orientation and platforms.

2. AMP: These are also known as Accelerated Mobile Pages. These are web development frameworks that are created to speed up the loading of the web pages on a mobile phone.

3. PWA: These are known as Progressive Web Apps. This is a type of application software which is delivered online and is built using technologies such as CSS, JavaScript, HTML etc. It is made to work on any platform that makes use of a standard compliant browser.

4. Landing Page: This is what appears when a user clicks on a PPC ad or a link from the search engine. The home page of a website is not the only landing page, any page of a website has potential to show up on the search engine results, so they all have potential to be landing pages.

5. CDN: Content Delivery Network is the globally distributed network of servers and centres of data. The main goal is to provide high performance and availability by distributing the severs accordingly to end users.

6. Firewall: This is a network security system that monitors and controls the network traffic based on certain security rules. This establishes a barrier between an internal network that is trusted and an external untrusted one such as the internet.

www.ingramcontent.com/pod-product-compliance
Lightning Source LLC
Chambersburg PA
CBHW020908180526
45163CB00007B/2668